A
MIND
OF
HIS OWN

In memory of my brother Jim Peterson.

A MIND OF HIS OWN

AN AUTOBIOGRAPHY

DAVID PETERSON

CONTENTS

INTRODUCTION

After assisting Mother in the composition of her "Memoirs," I decided to write my autobiography. It was a daunting task; however, the project was gratifying. Although an effort was made to include most significant events in my lifetime as well as the people involved in them, regrettably, some will have been overlooked.

The first step was to make a chronological list of major events, then fill in the blanks. Initially, much of the data came from memory, with each new thought triggering another. Every effort was made to be as accurate as possible, but memory is always a bit capricious and tenuous. Photographs, resumes and a Peace Corps journal were referenced. The greatest difficulty was determining what to include, or conversely, what to exclude. The result, at times, mirrors a travelogue as it chronicles a stint in the U.S. Peace Corps, one year exploring Europe, a career with two major airlines, and a lifetime of other trips and excursions around the world. I hope that the reader enjoys my journey and may gain some insight along the way.

An addendum includes two generations of my family tree, the epitaph of my Great-grandfather George Majors, and the Descriptions of Service documenting my participation as a Peace Corps volunteer in The Republic of Panama and as a Crisis Corps volunteer in the recovery effort in Louisiana for Hurricanes Katrina and Rita.

D.C.P.

Chapter 1

FAMILY AND ANCESTRY

On a winter evening, my mother, Vivian Peterson, went into labor while my father was trapping mink and muskrat. Dad made it home in time to drive "us" to the hospital. I came into the world around ten o'clock PM, Monday, November 22, 1943, in Melrose, Minnesota. Mother wrote in her "Memoirs" that "…this chubby little fellow had a mind of his own from the very beginning."

Edward Carl Peterson, my father, was born in Little Sauk, Todd County, Minnesota. He graduated from Sauk Centre High School in 1928 and attended Hamline University in Saint Paul, Minnesota. He served as a 2nd lieutenant in the Minnesota Army National Guard and was called to action during WWII. Illness kept him from going overseas. Nevertheless, he completed his tour of duty in Seattle, Washington.

When Dad returned to Minnesota, he began a career in the Sauk Centre Post Office and retired as an assistant postmaster. For more than thirty years he also served as a volunteer fireman. On the side, he kept busy doing carpentry in the community, a trade he learned from his father. I often helped him and was a good "go-fer." When he wasn't working at one of his jobs, he stayed busy in the yard or repairing something around the house. He built our boat house and a second garage. Dad was a role model in the community, an active member of the Methodist Church and a good father. He was a man of integrity who instilled me with honesty and sincerity. "Good enough is always your best," is something my father said to me when I was a teenager. I have always tried to put that counsel into practice.

Dad took me duck and pheasant hunting when I was a young boy. On one outing to hunt pheasants, before I was old enough to carry a gun, I accompanied Dad and his friend, Art MacDermond. I became lost after exiting a cornfield. We found each other following many anxious moments. Soon, I became a good marksman with a shotgun, a beautiful side-by-side — double barrel — A.H. Fox. On hunting trips, I learned to drive, taking advantage of the less traveled rural roads.

My brother Jim was discharged from the U.S. Coast Guard in the summer of 1959. He was stationed in Port Angeles, Washington. Dad arranged to deliver a pre-owned 1957 Cadillac, from a local dealership in Minnesota, to a dealer in Seattle. Together, we drove only during the day, so we saw much of the western countryside. I had my first driver's license and gained good driving experience. Dad was not used to power brakes and brought us to a screeching halt, one afternoon, at a Dairy Queen. He attracted everyone's attention and was embarrassed, but it did not prevent us from getting our desired treats.

We had our differences, particularly during high school years. We both put them behind us when I left for the University of Minnesota. Dad had difficulty expressing his emotions. There was one instance when he did not conceal them very well, and I almost misinterpreted them. He visited me at Pioneer Hall at the U of M. We had a long conversation in my dormitory room where he shared how proud he was of me. He shed some tears, and I unwittingly asked if he had something in his eyes. He quietly said that everything was okay as he dried his eyes. After many years of confinement in different facilities, Dad died of Alzheimer's disease, January 13, 1999.

Vivian Jane Coons, my mother, was born in Getty Township, Stearns County, Minnesota. She also graduated from Sauk Centre High School in 1928 (she skipped a grade in country school), and attended Saint Cloud Teachers College. Appendicitis kept her from completing her studies. She later enrolled in a business school in Minneapolis.

Mother was a matriarch who devoted her life to the family, but also had a working career. She found time to do everything, and I do not know how she managed. In addition to her responsibilities as a homemaker, she worked as a clerk at the Mary Ann Shop and at J C Penny's and, lastly, as a supervisor at the Minnesota Home School for Girls, a state correctional institution in Sauk Centre. Her additional income helped clothe and feed us and allowed us to have things we would otherwise have done without. My brother Bob and I would not have been able to have orthodontics if she had not worked. She epitomized patience, tolerance and understanding. Mother was an active member of the Methodist Church and played the organ and piano when necessary.

Those were days when socks were darned by hand; clothes were washed, hung outside to dry and ironed. Mother even pressed sheets and pillowcases using a mangling iron. She raised chickens. That remains a vivid memory because one Bantam rooster used to chase me around the yard. Mother was always available, supportive and encouraging. She was an excellent driver and our chauffeur until we were old enough to drive. She drove us to The Cities (Minneapolis-Saint Paul) where we rode street cars and shopped at Dayton's and Donaldson's department stores. At Christmas, we marveled at decorations in Minneapolis.

Mother was adventurous, loved the outdoors, hunted and camped. She had a flower garden, liked to rake leaves and enjoyed mowing the lawn on a riding mower. At age 86 she rode on a Jet Ski! Both Dad and Mother were avid sports fans. They attended high school basketball and football games and football games at the University of Minnesota. On TV, they watched the Minneapolis Lakers, the Minnesota Twins and Vikings. They went to sportsman's shows at the Minneapolis Amory. Mother became excited when watching a sporting event, whether in person or on television. Occasionally, one or two expletives were heard during a tense moment or when the outcome was disappointing.

Although Vivian was her given name, she was also known as "Did" by everyone related to her on her brother's side (Uncle Carol). Mother said that her nickname originated as a result of her cousin Grace

3

Lamb not being able to say "Viv." Isabel Coons, her sister-in-law (and high school classmate), had the unusual nickname of "Tib" or "Tibby," given to her by her schoolmates. Its origin came from a poem written by Robert Burns, "O Tibby, I hae seen the day," inscribed to a lady named Isabella. Nonetheless, we all knew who was being addressed when we heard "Did," "Aunt Did," "Tib" or "Tibby."

In 1992, Mother gave up her lake home where she remained alone after Dad was confined to an Alzheimer's facility. When she realized that caring for her home was more than she could handle, she and Cammee (her Siamese cat) moved into an apartment in town. After ten years, she relocated to an apartment at Lakeshore Estates on Sauk Lake. It offered many essential amenities that made her life easier. Meals were provided daily and it had an elevator, a beauty parlor, a chapel and many of her friends lived there.

We talked by phone every weekend and, more often, if there were something special to share or a question that required an answer, especially, when we were writing her "Memoirs." That document is a wonderful insight into her heartfelt reflections representing her childhood up to her final years. Inevitably, we discussed genealogy. For three days during one visit, we labeled old family photographs. Each one had a story of its own. We found one of Dad standing next to his first car, a Willis. It was always a pleasure to be in her company.

Vivian & Edward Peterson – Wedding – November 17, 1935

My siblings and I made up the rest of the Peterson family. We were born approximately three years apart. James Edward was born first, Karen Jane second, I (David Carol) third, Carol Sue and Robert Lowell — twins — fourth and fifth. The twins were a big surprise. Dad had a vasectomy sometime after my birth that obviously was not the sophisticated procedure of today. Doctor Kettlewell, the family physician and friend, covered their health expenses until they were eighteen.

Jim was six years older, however, our paths crossed frequently throughout our lifetime. After graduating from high school, he served in the U.S. Coast Guard for ten years. He retired prematurely from the Coast Guard with a medical discharge resulting from a knee injury. Jim then worked his way up through the U.S. Postal Service and retired as a postmaster. He resided most of his life in Minnesota, at times turning down opportunities elsewhere, in order to be close to our aging parents. His first marriage was to Mary Klas. They had a daughter and son, Jane Marie and James Scott. Memories of Jim and Mary are many, including boating on Lake of the Woods and playing cards. Mary and her sisters were enthusiastic card players. We played our favorite game of 500, often past midnight. Jim later married Gail Gruse Nelson. They moved to a quaint little Sears house on Walnut Street in Sauk Centre.

Jim was diagnosed with stage 4 non-Hodgkin's lymphoma (MCL: mantle cell lymphoma) in the fall of 2010. To make a very painful story short, he had a stem cell transplant, followed by years of chemotherapy that gave him a new lease on life. During those years an incredible bond developed between Jim, Gail and me. After nearly ten years, his body finally gave out on September 05, 2019.

The last four years of Jim's life were very meaningful for me. We always enjoyed each other's company, but grew substantially closer during his physical decline. He was extremely frustrated at not being able to help others and do manual things he was accustomed to doing. Accepting help was, at first, met with reluctance. It was heartbreaking to see him in that manner. However, his condition created many opportunities for me to be of help.

With considerable frequency that included two or more weeks at a time, I helped Jim and Gail in every way I could either in Minnesota or their winter home in Florida. I had the pleasure of driving them to and from their two homes. The drive each way took four to five days in their motor home, allowing for time to build on our feelings, interests and experiences. It was a time filled with merriment as well. In Florida, several days were devoted to reopening their home that had been closed for months. The reverse was done in spring when it was time to go back to Minnesota. Diversions included Jim's favorite pastime: motoring the pontoon through canals and on lakes. I was fortunate to have several years of quality time with them. Gail and Jim shared an unconditional love for each other.

Karen was our resident musician (although all five of us played musical instruments). She was an accomplished pianist and organist and also played the oboe. She was the organist at the Methodist Church. Karen attended Hamline University in Saint Paul, Minnesota, after graduating from high school. However, she opted to pursue an airline career as a flight attendant that lasted nearly thirty years, first with Braniff International, followed by Alaska Airlines. She traveled to many parts of the globe and flew military charters to Vietnam during that war. Her airline career ended prematurely due to a deteriorating eye condition (cone rod dystrophy). Karen never complains about her vision loss. On the contrary, she remains positive, accepts the challenge of dealing with her handicap, and with little difficulty navigates her way in Minneapolis. Sadly, she can no longer do her favorite things: sewing and playing the organ and piano. Like her mother, she is caring, kind and generous. Our lives have overlapped continuously, especially during our airline careers.

My first three years transpired across the street from the Methodist Church, a stone's throw to the Great Northern railroad tracks. Frequently, Karen calmed me when trains — especially the noisy steam locomotives — passed by. Yes, there were steam engines when I was a child! Although I was too young to remember living in that large white house, I saw it for many years when attending services at the Methodist Church.

It was a definite disadvantage being a middle child no matter how hard my parents may have tried to prevent it. The older two had needs that required attention: being driven to extracurricular events and jobs, for example. The younger two demanded extra care due their age. The resulting separation made me very independent. I made my own decisions or sought answers elsewhere.

Sue lived most of her life in Minnesota. She owned a hardware store in Redwood Falls with her husband, Don Vance, before their retirement. Sue had her share of obstacles too: breast cancer, a broken pelvis and CLL (chronic lymphocytic leukemia). She does not feel sorry for herself and instead has a positive outlook. Sue is a perceptive person and one who likes to be "in charge." She never hesitates to offer her opinion, looks at the big picture and has an uncanny ability to handle any situation. Her only child is Lori Lynn from her first marriage to Bill Schurman. Sue and Don spend summers at their cabin near Leech Lake in north central Minnesota and winter in Florida.

David Peterson

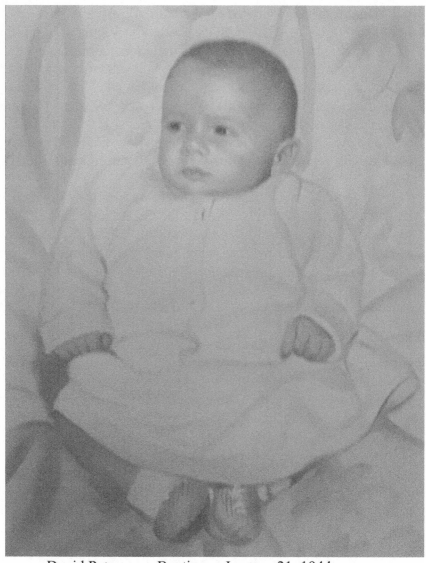

David Peterson – Baptism – January 21, 1944
First Methodist Church, Sauk Centre, Minnesota

8

Bob graduated from Saint Cloud State University. He married Lesalyn Ferrel and for more than thirty years they lived in Wisconsin. Both were elementary school teachers. Their home was close to the Saint Croix National Scenic Riverway and the Minnesota and Wisconsin Interstate Park — a great place for boating and hiking — that offered stunning views of the Saint Croix River. In the years before their divorce, Bob, Les and I shared many happy times. Regrettably, Bob's increasing conservatism and strong religious beliefs put a strain on our relationship. In retirement, Les turned to painting and moved to California. Three of her paintings hang in my dining room. Bob remained in Wisconsin and later married Nancy Rasmussen.

Only two grandparents lived long enough for me to know well: Granny Arvilla Elizabeth Lamb (maternal) and Grandpa Olaf Peterson (paternal). Arvilla's husband, Ulysses Coons, died when I was about three. My fondest memory of Grandfather Ulysses is sitting with him in a rocking chair. Mother said he sang to me when I was on his lap. Perhaps that is why I became fond of rockers. Olaf's wife, Grandmother Leah Ada Drager, died when Dad was a young man.

Granny lived with us several years and died when I was in high school. She was a delightful, proud and proper lady. She was well read and kept up with current events, including high school activities. Granny was a big help to Mother, especially caring for the twins. For many years, during winter, she flew to Savannah, Georgia to be with her son, Carol.

One morning, during the Korean War, I remember going to the mailbox to get the *Minneapolis Morning Tribune.* The headlines described North Koreans advancing on Bunker Hill. I ran into the house, probably crying, to show Granny the headlines. She assured me that it was not the Bunker Hill near where our friends (the Bunkers) lived but one many miles away in Korea.

It was entertaining to watch Granny leave with her friends in their "old" cars. Barbara Engle would race the engine as she backed out of the driveway. Mother said that Mrs. Engle believed that everyone else should watch out for her. Maude Fielding drove one of those four-door black "boxes" that used a crank to start the engine. Was it a Model T Ford? Mother alleged that Maude was a safer driver than Mrs. Engle.

I liked going to Uncle Alvin (Granny's brother) and Mary Lamb's house. Mary made popcorn balls that she covered in chocolate. Granny was close to her brother. Alvin's daughter Grace lived there during most summer months when she was not teaching high school in Brainerd. She entertained us with stories about our families. I often referenced the abundant genealogy data she collected.

It was a sad day when Granny left us to live in the Sarepta Home. She fell in our house when only the twins and I were home. We were unable to lift her up, so I called neighbors to assist us. The Warnekes were there in minutes. Shortly after, at her insistence, Granny moved to a nursing home. It was a melancholy time for Mother, but it was what Granny wanted.

Grandpa Olaf was a tall slender man who always wore a suit and, most often, a hat. He made his livelihood as a carpenter, teaching many of his skills to my father. Several homes that he built still stand in the Sauk Centre area. His older brother, Peter Lystad, was born on a ship en route to America. Peter kept his mother's maiden name as his surname. According to his daughter, he claimed that "there were too many Petersons in Minnesota!" Dad and I drove to visit Grandpa when he was in the Struxness Nursing Home in Belgrade, often bringing him to our home for the day.

As a family, we have been spread across the country, still remained close-knit. Mother and Dad did an excellent job of including us in their lives. In later years, they continued that tradition and traveled to wherever we were living.

November 17, 1985 marked my parents' fiftieth wedding anniversary. We five children were able to help plan their celebration at the Methodist Church. They renewed their wedding vows in the sanctuary followed by a reception in the dining area. At times, Dad was confused and did not recognize everyone, even postal employees that he had worked with, due to the early onset of Alzheimer's.

Vivian Peterson with her five children – 1992
Bob, Karen, Jim, Sue & David

Paddling a canoe down Sauk River with Mother and Karen in July 1994 was extraordinary. Indeed, it was one of the grandest times we three had together. (Jim and I did the groundwork the summer before, covering the twenty miles from Sauk Centre to Melrose in about 4 ½ hours helped by a strong current.) The scenery was beautiful. There was abundant wildlife: animals we could hear but not see, huge fish and a variety of birds and ducks. Mother sat on a cushion in the middle of the canoe, Karen paddled in the front, and I navigated from the back. It was often a comedy of errors that made it hard to control our laughter during difficult negotiations in the winding river. One comical incident happened when the two women struggled to exit the canoe, nearly tipping it over.

At age 93 (May 2003), Mother had a partial knee replacement. Due to pain, she was losing her ability to walk. Her excellent health qualified her for the procedure. The surgery restored her quality of life and, for many more years, she walked at her leisure with no difficulty.

Karen devoted more than a month of her time to assist Mother during the long recuperation period. Without her presence, Mother's recovery would have been longer and without the comfort of her own home. To express our appreciation, Sue, Don and I had a cedar chest restored that Mother had given Karen. Uncle Carol handmade the chest and inlaid Mother's initials — V J C — on the lid.

Mother continued marching along. We thought 95 was a banner year. Then followed 96, 97, 98, 99, 100 and 101 years! Her centennial birthday — January 01, 2011 — was a huge celebration at the nursing home where she resided. More than 100 people came to celebrate on that bitter cold day in Sauk Centre. Alas, on March 20, 2012, Vivian Peterson quietly succumbed to old age, with Karen, Sue and me at her side.

The following are impressions of my boyhood town. Sauk Centre was a close-knit community with a population about 3,500 in the center of the state. Its name derived from the Sauk Indian tribe combined with its geographical location. It served as a hub for the rural agricultural area that supported a thriving downtown. Both Great Northern and Northern Pacific Railroads passed through town. Great Northern still operated passenger trains into the 1960s. The tracks were removed and replaced by the Lake Wobegon Trail, part of the Rails-to-Trails program. Originally, the 29-mile-long macadam biking and hiking pathway extended from Avon to Sauk Centre. Eventually, it expanded to several hundred miles across central Minnesota.

Sauk Centre was the birthplace of author Sinclair Lewis who wrote *Main Street*. The community became well known after Lewis won the Nobel Prize for Literature in 1930. Oversized street signs were erected in his honor: ORIGINAL MAIN STREET and SINCLAIR LEWIS AVENUE. The high school mascot is Mainstreeters.

The town was typical of Main Street America. When walking down a street, at least one person was known and, more often, several familiar faces were seen. It was clean and bustling. Businesses included a J C Penny store, a Sears, a Ben Franklin "five and dime" store, several taverns, gas stations, car dealers, two drug stores and many eating establishments. The public schools were located downtown. A post office and library were on Main Street. Our home was located three miles from the traffic light at the corner of Main Street and Sinclair Lewis Avenue. Trips to town were often on foot or by bicycle and, in summer months, it was not unusual to go by motorboat, as the town and our home were on the shores of Sauk Lake.

At Christmas, decorations lit up the lamp posts and lighted garlands hung across the two main streets. Each garland had a huge ornament hanging from the center. It was a busy little community during the holidays, as most people shopped in the local stores.

An on-going project of mine involved researching family genealogy. Many more ancestors have been discovered since the onset; however, there was too much data to include here. Instead, the following paragraphs briefly include an accounting of that investigation. My genealogical research began in the 1970s and was set aside until August 2003. That year, I opened a can of worms when I made inquiries regarding some of my ancestors.

Paternal ancestors have been traced back ten generations to German Grandfathers Christian Drager and Martin Gelbert. Much information is missing on Grandfather Olaf Peterson's ancestry. Cousins Virginia Freda Drager, Evelyn Drager Judes and Janet Johnson Izzo contributed data from their research.

I am a descendent of some interesting people, including George Majors and possibly Henry Hudson. George Majors (my great-great-great-great-great grandfather) was a Hessian soldier in the Revolutionary War who joined the American cause. In Vermont, a national cemetery was established in his honor. Henry Hudson is believed to be an uncle seven times removed. He was captain of the ship *Discovery* that sailed in search of the Northwest Passage. Hudson Bay was named in his honor.

On the maternal side, a great deal was discovered regarding the Coons, thanks to cousins Gary E. Coons, Judy Coons Peterson and Joyce Coons Fasano. Documentation indicates that Great-great-great-great-great-great-grandfather Matthias Kuntz was born in 1660 in Germany.

In 2010, a wealth of information was added to the Lamb ancestry, thanks to a Danish woman, Annelise Nielsen Wichmann. My sister Sue traveled with me to Denmark, homeland of our ancestors, the Nielsens (Nelsons in America). Annelise (no relation) presented me with a binder that goes back 13 generations to Great-grandfather Niels Raa born in 1555. We toured the village of Borre on the island of Mon where the Nielsens lived and attended a Sunday service in their church, Borre Kirke.

Noteworthy ancestors include the Fairbanks and Lambs. The Fairbanks House (in Dedham, Massachusetts), named after Jonathan Fairbanks, was built in 1636 and is the oldest wooden frame house in America. Robert Morris, a Lamb relative, came to America from England. He was a delegate to the Continental Congress and signed the Declaration of Independence. A descendent of his, also named Robert Morris (from Oxford, Mississippi and a Doctor of Law and Philosophy), founded the Order of the Eastern Star. John Fawcett, an English philosopher related through the Lambs, wrote the poem "Blest Be the Tie That Binds" that was set to a famous hymn tune.

The countries that represent my forebears are Denmark, England, Germany and Norway. It appears that my ancestry consists of the following: Dane = 2/16, English = 5/16, German = 5/16 and Norwegian = 4/16. Norwegian is etched on family gravestones in Long Bridge Cemetery in Todd County, Minnesota. (The Danes allege that I am all Danish since Norway was at one time part of Denmark.) In any event, I am 6/16 Scandinavian. Mother always claimed I was a duke's mixture!

Chapter 2

GROWING UP ON SAUK LAKE

Our home sat on a desirable site on the eastern shore of Sauk Lake. It was ideal for observing beautiful sunsets, but we could also watch storms blow across the lake from the west. (Sauk Lake is nine miles long and about two miles wide.) Dad built a dock and raft for our summer pleasure. Nearly every free moment involved boating, fishing, swimming or water skiing. It was a very popular place for our friends, young and old alike. Our house was always full of visitors. My parents were very accommodating to our friends who sometimes tracked through the house with wet feet and dripping swimsuits.

The lake home started out as a cabin built by Dad and Grandpa Olaf. They transformed the "cottage" — as it was fondly called — into a larger house to accommodate our family of seven. We were crowded and had only one bathroom, however, we managed and learned to share.

There was much work to do in our expansive tree-filled yard. Dad strove to keep it immaculate, with our help, of course. There was a lawn to mow, leaves to rake and a shoreline to keep clean. We also maintained a large vegetable and flower garden. The garden provided us with a variety of fresh vegetables. Mother kept a full cellar of canned items. My favorite were beets and bread and butter pickles. We were proud of our home and willingly helped to preserve it.

The property covered approximately eight acres along the lake shore that provided a great source of entertainment. It was densely wooded on both sides of the cottage where the manicured lawn ended.

The woods were a haven for animals and plants that provided a perfect place to play. We built forts out of tree branches, made bows and arrows, played hide and seek, climbed trees and watched fish from high above on the clay banks overlooking the lake. A well-worn winding path connected to the house of our parents' best friends, Art and Ann MacDermond. Mother and Dad ultimately gave each of us a one-acre lake shore lot.

Peterson home – Summer 1965

Dogs and cats were perpetual family members. Irish Setters were Dad's breed of choice that he trained for hunting. Male dogs were named Sandy. At times, there was a black Labrador, in addition to a setter. One spring, our three female cats all had a litter about the same time. We were permitted to watch them grow until they could be on their own, then we gave them to a nearby farmer. Midnight was our favorite cat and the longest living pet. She was black as pitch except for one tiny white spot on her chest. My cat was black with white socks. I named her Mittens.

For several years, the road past our house was gravel. One of our pranks was to place a purse attached to a string, covered with gravel, and hide in the ditch waiting for a car to come along. When someone stopped to pick up the purse, we pulled the string and ran. The dirt road had a downside: it raised dust. That became an issue when Mother hung washing outside to dry. If there were a wind, or it changed direction, dust soiled the damp clothes. The day finally arrived to pave the road. Being typical kids, we played in piles of gravel that were mixed with tar. Mother resorted to kerosene to remove stubborn tar that covered us from head to toe.

The family camped throughout Minnesota but mostly at Lake of the Woods. Family friends (the Pickets) moved from Sauk Centre to Baudette that provided an added enticement to go to northern Minnesota. It offered an opportunity to hunt ducks, grouse and deer, fish on Lake of the Woods and Rainy River, pick blueberries and explore the beautiful wilderness. I once accompanied Harlan Picket, a state game warden, to blow up a beaver dam that caused flooding.

There were road trips to Georgia, Florida and California. Mother's only sibling, Uncle Carol, lived in Savannah. Dad's sister Ethel Johnson lived in Miami and his sister Dorothy Freedland lived in Long Beach. Those trips were inexpensive because we camped along the way or drove straight through to our destination. They were educational excursions that offered an opportunity to see the United States. (Eventually, I visited all 50 states, Puerto Rico, Guam and the U.S. Virgin Islands.)

The first long distance trip that I can remember was when I was about five years old. In 1949, nine of us rode to Savannah in a green four-door Plymouth that included Granny and Mary Lamb. We must have been packed in like sardines. The return trip was easier, as Mary stayed in Savannah with her son, Donald. From Pittsburgh, I had a vivid memory of yellow smoke billowing from factories. Whenever we encountered road construction and saw graders, I thought each one was driven by Adolph Ebensteiner who plowed snow on the road past our house.

Minnesota winters apparently produced more snow than today. We dug tunnels, made forts and climbed huge banks of snow piled along the roadside from the plows. Skiing, sledding and tobogganing were other winter activities. That was before the influx of snowmobiles. Even Mother snow-skied, often towed behind a car. Across the road was a hill that led to a frozen pond. It was exciting to sled down the hill and slide across the ice, having tied up the barbed wire fence so we could safely maneuver beneath it without snagging our coats.

Ice skating was my favorite winter sport. The City maintained good rinks for skating and hockey. Some winters, Sauk Lake froze over smoothly that made it ideal for skating before it became snow-covered. One could literally skate for miles on the glass-like surface. The lake was also ideal for ice fishing. "Villages" of fish houses were located above the good fishing areas. Originally, most fish houses had few amenities, often only a small stove for heat. Jim and I enjoyed many hours ice fishing on the nearby lakes. In spring, as the ice broke up, we carefully floated on huge chunks of ice along the shore using a stick or a pole to guide us. We prayed that we would not fall into the cold water.

Peterson home – Winter 1960

Chapter 3

CHILDHOOD STORIES

One story that was certainly not a favorite memory, at the time, occurred when Mother went by Greyhound to visit Dad who was stationed in Seattle with the National Guard. Karen and Jim stayed with other families. However, I was placed in the care of the MacDermonds. Although I was old enough to walk and could sleep in my own bed at home, they made me sleep in a *crib*!

We shopped at S.P. Hansen's grocery store owned by in-laws: parents of Aunt Tib. I have no idea of my age, yet I was tall enough to reach into a large ceramic jar to scoop a handful of salted peanuts. One day, Mother caught me in the act and offered to pay for my "crime." Jean Hansen showed no concern. To me, it never occurred that I had done something wrong, but that was the last time I reached into that jar.

When I was about 10 years old, our front picture window that overlooked the lake served as an excellent lookout to spot imaginary enemy invaders. Bob and Sue were armed with toy pistols. I had a BB gun that was presumed empty. I fired, and a small hole appeared in the righthand corner of the window. There was no punishment. Dad did not replace the window, instead he patched the tiny hole and left it as a reminder. A lesson learned.

Merle Pangburn lived on a farm about a mile from our house. She raised riding horses and other livestock. Sue, Bob and I devoted many hours helping her and enjoyed the benefit of riding her horses. We drove her cattle down the road to "the eighty" where they would pasture for the day. Pal, an Indian Paint that loved to swim, was my favorite horse. Pal and I made frequent trips to the lake for a swim. Sometimes she would unexpectedly lie down in standing water, drenching the rider. We helped deliver calves, and Sue was the expert in that area. Merle was kind both to people and to her animals. She was a bright woman who liked solving crossword puzzles. My last memory of Merle was driving her around Sauk Lake one autumn day when I was home from the university. Foliage colors were spectacular, and she thoroughly enjoyed the ride. I snapped a precious photo of her.

The Triscos owned farmland across the road. Their home was about two miles away — as the crow flies — through woods, pasture and cornfields. Two of their children were the same age as Karen and me. Often, a Holstein bull hastened our journey when we cut the corner of the pasture, forcing us to quickly crawl under the barbed wire fence to escape. In the barn, we swung from ropes in the loft and dropped onto mounds of hay. We played "Kick the Can" and "Annie, Annie, Over."

I found farm life exciting. I preferred to drive a tractor, particularly their old John Deere, pulling a large hay wagon during threshing season while men loaded heavy bales onto the wagon. At times, I helped milk their Holstein cows.

Mrs. Trisco added the term "forenoon" to my vocabulary. She asked me to return "in the forenoon" the following day to help with chores. I promptly showed up at *noon* the next day. She kindly explained its meaning: morning, or the early part of the day ending at noon.

Mary Gritzmacher and I virtually grew up together. We were the same age. She lived "next door:" a half mile up the hill and around the corner by road, or in shouting distance along the lake. A substantial amount of our summers was consumed on or near the lake. We skipped school for "important" alternatives (such as attending a state basketball tournament when a neighboring town competed), went roller skating at the Sauk Centre Coliseum and danced at New Munich's ballroom. We had many mutual friends and often found ourselves at the same parties or going to the same events.

Merle Pangburn – Sauk Centre – Autumn 1965

Chapter 4

SAUK CENTRE HIGH SCHOOL

Sauk Centre High School was large enough to offer a broad curriculum and still be competitive both academically and in sports. Still, it was small enough that one could participate in several extracurricular activities. My junior year, the basketball team won third place at the State tournament, truly a feat for our small school. That was before divisions were established based on school enrollment.

Because I lived three miles from the school, I rode on one of those long yellow buses. The ride *to* school was short, about twenty minutes. The ride *home*, depending on the route taken by the driver, often lasted an hour, or more. To my recollection, there were no major incidents on the bus, even though it was chock-a-block with students. Mary Gritzmacher and I drove to school, in her car, our junior and senior years. We often arrived at our seats in the band room as the bell was ringing (band practice was our first class). Mr. Raitor usually looked the other way, unless we were too late, requiring an excuse from the principal's office.

I was a percussionist in the concert and marching bands that provided an opportunity to participate in concerts, parades, trips and band camp at Bemidji State College (now Bemidji State University). For a while, Karen and I were in the band at the same time. After she graduated, the twins and I were in the band together. The band traveled to community celebrations, sporting events and competitions. The drum ensemble won first place at state, my senior year. At Bemidji State band camp, I was selected to play in the honor band. I participated in the City Band that gave weekly concerts in the bandshell at the park.

Every fall, the marching band attended the University of Minnesota Band Day at a Gopher football game. During one unforgettable game, we were drenched by a rainstorm that soaked our old maroon uniforms made of wool, turning our under clothing and skin the color of our uniforms. When I was a senior, Dr. Frank Bencriscutto, the U of M band director, was guest conductor for our annual concert. When he learned that I intended to enroll at the U of M, he encouraged me to audition for a spot in the Minnesota Marching Band.

I enjoyed the role of photographer for the *O-Sa-Ge*, the school annual. It was an excellent introduction to photography, a skill that I have used my entire life. In addition, I wrote for the school paper *The Mainstreeter*. I acted in school plays and competed in speech contests. One of my biggest thrills was winning the district speech contest for serious interpretation. I enjoyed sports, nevertheless, had little interest in participating in organized sports, much to Dad's chagrin. I liked tennis and swimming; however, they were not offered at SCHS. I took courses in both at the U of M.

Two classmates that made lasting impressions were Nobu Moriwaki and Andrew Lesser. Nobu was an exchange student from Tokyo, Japan. She had a cheerful disposition and provided an insight into a culture of which we were very naïve. Our school annual was dedicated to Nobu and in memory of Andy. Andy was killed one evening while working at a filling station during our senior year. Our friendship began in kindergarten when we rode the bus to and from school.

I interacted with many schoolmates, including those from other classes, due to my involvement in various organizations. One evening, two buddies introduced me to Southern Comfort. We drank right from the bottle! It was a painful lesson. Karen came to the rescue and held my head over the toilet during my agony. We told Mother it was a case of stomach flu, but I doubt that we fooled her.

On a winter night, after a basketball game, nine of us were riding in one car and were broadsided by another vehicle. Two of us were slightly injured. My bleeding head wound looked worse than it was because blood had frozen on my face. Judy Corrigan rode in an ambulance and the state police drove me to the hospital. Our injuries were minor: contusions, cracked ribs and cuts requiring sutures. For a while, it hurt us both to laugh. Mother and Dad were relieved to learn that I was okay and had not been driving their car. The consolation was that our team won and the other driver was determined to be at fault.

Only a few instructors made a significant impact on me. Alan Juelke was a 9th grade advisor who taught science. His inspiration resulted in me receiving the highest score on the final exam. Charlotte Hedin taught sophomore English. She was well prepared and took interest in her students. Laurence Casserly taught English, Latin and was the *O-Sa-Ge* advisor. I was a band member under the instruction of Alan Raitor who taught choral and instrumental music. The music program made huge strides under his direction.

A favorite place to congregate after school and athletic events, was the Main Street Café, a large restaurant with booths and a counter. Another popular place was the Corner Drug store. The soda fountain was always teeming with students. Gail Gruse, my future sister-in-law, worked there.

Whenever I was not involved in a school activity, part-time work kept me busy after school and on weekends: mowing lawns, delivering bread for Nelson's Bakery and custodial work at the Methodist Church. I inherited the janitor job at the Methodist Church after Jim graduated. On occasion, I would clean "in time" to music when Karen (the church organist) practiced. For two years, I did multiple tasks for Charlie Corrigan's funeral home. His daughter Judy was a classmate. We found mischief whenever her parents were away. She often had friends over to party in their finished attic. My last job, before I left for the University of Minnesota, was as a City lifeguard.

Working at a turkey farm was the dirtiest, most irrational job I had during high school. Two classmates and I accepted that job "on a lark." For one week, we reported to the farm at 4:00 AM during the cooler hours. As we caught the turkeys and loaded them onto tractor trailers, we were scratched and bruised by the huge birds that gobbled, kicked and flapped their wings. For days, I tasted dust and dreamed of turkeys. Moreover, I was allergic to dust!

SCHS had its first All School Reunion in 1990. However, the second Reunion, in 1995, was most memorable. The Petersons, apart from Dad (who was in an Alzheimer's facility), were all together. Mother, Jim and Karen were living in Sauk Centre. Because our community and school were small, we knew many people other than those from our own class. In the parade, as a representative of her 1928 class, Mother rode in a classic car of the same year! It was a good time to reunite with classmates. Mary, Russ and I met at their Big Birch Lake cabin and took their pontoon to the Rock Tavern for dinner. Brother Jim met his future wife Gail, at that reunion. Gail's sister Sue (my friend and classmate) and I *may* have had some influence in that meeting!

Chapter 5

THE UNIVERSITY OF MINNESOTA

The five years I attended the University of Minnesota proved very fulfilling. It was more than a period of personal enlightenment. In addition to the knowledge I acquired, it provided time to challenge, experiment, make new acquaintances, mature and contemplate. Although attending the U of M cost more, was farther from home and had a huge enrollment compared to smaller nearby state colleges, it offered more opportunities, including a chance to participate in the Minnesota Marching Band.

The Minneapolis campus was one of the largest in the United States with a student enrollment in excess of 40,000. The size was one of its biggest attractions, along with its inherent diversity. Mother and Sue were both students while I was there. Mother attended classes at the Extension Division, taking courses related to her position at the Minnesota State School. Sue was a student until love changed her plans. Two high school classmates, Dick Schwartz and Mary Gritzmacher, also attended the U of M. Russ Sieben, Mary's husband and high school sweetheart, were married in the summer of 1963. He was a pre-dental student a year ahead of us. He helped us through the complicated registration procedure. Mary and I enrolled in several classes together.

I liked all Spanish classes, my major field. Ironically, I exerted little effort to study Latin in high school, yet enthusiastically accepted the challenge to learn Spanish. Each year the Spanish Department produced a play. I participated my junior year and assumed a leading role, *Jefe de Administración* (Administration Manager), in *El Tintero* (*The Inkwell*) by

Carlos Muñiz. Social studies was my minor field. I enjoyed the required courses in economics, history and sociology but not statistics. I received my worst passing grade in that course. It did not help that I took it during a summer while working fulltime. Three favorite elective courses were cultural anthropology, astronomy and geology. Russ and I took the anthropology class together.

Introduction to Psychology was the largest class with an enrollment of more than one thousand students each quarter. The course was required for all university students. Lectures were held in Northrop Auditorium. The Minnesota Multiphasic Personality Inventory, one of the most commonly used psychological tests in the world, was administered during the course. (The test was developed by clinical psychologist Starke Hathaway and neuropsychiatrist J.C. McKinley, two faculty members at the University of Minnesota. The MMPI was created to be a tool for mental health professionals to help diagnose mental health disorders.)

Early one winter morning, on my way to that class, I slipped on ice outside the dormitory and landed in a puddle of water in front of a multitude of students. I was unhurt but embarrassed, laughed along with everyone else, picked up my soggy books and returned to my room. I had another calamity involving that same class. Just shy of entering Northrop Auditorium, a bird dropped its "load" on my head. It must have been a big bird too. To make matters worse, at that time I had thick brown hair covering my head. I found the nearest washroom to clean up, then returned to the dormitory, having decided that it was an omen not to attend psychology that day.

For four years, I lived on-campus in Pioneer Hall, the only co-ed residence hall. Dormitory living offered many benefits, but the most important was experiencing the vibrant student atmosphere. One diversion for students involved going to Stub and Herbs, a local pub a few blocks from the dorm. It offered a place to unwind after exams, on weekends and after football games. Although many pitchers of beer were consumed, in those days there was little, if any, binge drinking. Instead, we drank as an outlet or chance to socialize. Gerry Gau, Diane Erickson, Ginny Holland and I "relaxed" there.

As a dormitory resident, I took advantage of employment opportunities offered in Pioneer Hall. In order to pay for my education, I worked nearly fulltime. I made a commitment to put myself through college that was a way of asserting independence. (My parents only needed to supplement the first quarter of my university expenses.) During my freshman year I helped the kitchen staff. The first quarter I washed dishes, and the remaining two quarters I prepared breakfast, reporting at 5:30 AM. In the ensuing three years, I held a coveted switchboard operator position, and the last year I was promoted to senior clerk in charge of front desk operations, including the switchboard. Private telephones were provided in all rooms by the time I graduated, although office personnel were still required to handle mail and other duties.

During Christmas breaks I worked as a temporary assistant at the Minneapolis Post Office. Dad arranged for those positions through his postal contacts. In the summer of my junior year, three of us rented a house near campus and worked as custodians at University Hospitals. Without doubt, the number of hours dedicated to supplementing my income had an impact on my studies and ultimately my grades. Due to my busy schedule, I seldom went home. I rode home on a Great Northern passenger train when time permitted.

Following my freshman year, I was hired as the waterfront director at Robert's Pine Beach Resort, an exclusive operation on Gull Lake near Brainerd, Minnesota. I was responsible for teaching sailing, giving rides in the Cheerio — a beautiful wooden inboard Chris Craft built in the 1940s — and helping with fishing boats. Fishermen paid me twenty-five cents to clean each fish, so I learned to fillet very fast and expertly. A young woman who recently lost her husband to cancer seduced me on a Cheerio outing. As we were prohibited from fraternizing with guests, her mother requested that the owner grant me permission to spend time with her after hours. He consented. We went out to dinner and to movies and, admittedly, she expanded my knowledge of the "birds and the bees." Experience teaches!

My freshman and sophomore years I was privileged to participate in the drumline of the Minnesota Marching Band. MMB was made up of 144 men in "the block," 10 men carrying flags representing each Big Ten university (that was before Maryland, Nebraska, Penn State and Rutgers joined the conference) and a drum major (no women were in the band until the 1970s). Our rehearsals were very demanding. Every afternoon, at 3:30 PM we "stepped off" promptly to a drum cadence and marched to the practice field. We rehearsed until 6:30 PM, or later, and again the morning of the game. The hard work paid off, above all, when we marched onto the field at Memorial Stadium to resounding cheers of fans.

We wore our band caps *backwards* many times in those days. Reversing caps when your team was victorious became a tradition that allegedly originated at a Minnesota vs. Michigan football game. Michigan band members said they would be wearing their caps backwards following their victory. Joyfully, the Minnesota band marched off the field that day with their plumes at the back and the team proudly carried the Little Brown Jug trophy. *Minnesota, Hats Off to Thee*!

MMB traveled to other universities for football games and participated in special events. It had a unique reputation as a "singing band." Marching down the street, in restaurants and other public places, we sang university songs in four-part harmony, including "Hail, Minnesota!" and John Phillip Sousa's "Minnesota March." Dr. Frank Bencrisciutto — "Dr. Ben" to the MMB members — turned MMB into one of the premier marching bands in the country.

I took advantage of a perk offered to band members: free tickets to the Minneapolis Symphony Orchestra (now the Minnesota Orchestra). Concerts were performed on-campus in Northrop Auditorium. It was an excellent introduction to classical music by that renowned ensemble.

David Peterson

President John F. Kennedy was assassinated on my birthday, November 22, 1963. When I returned to the dorm from classes, I switched on the radio — no TVs in our rooms — to hear the voice of Walter Cronkite announce that the President had been shot. Soon my room filled with students as we listened to updates. Everyone was in total disbelief when we heard Walter say, "...the President is dead." That event will always be remembered as the most distressing of my lifetime.

I studied in Jalapa, México at the *Universidad Veracruzana* (Veracruz University) during my junior year. Two friends from Pioneer Hall, Dennis Dvoracek and Jeff Payant, were enrolled in the program too. We rented a car to drive from Minneapolis to Texas. We stopped in San Antonio to see the Alamo and in the town of West to visit Dennis' relatives. At Nuevo Laredo, we continued by bus to Jalapa.

It was a good program that would have a lasting influence on me. Dennis and I lived with the López family. Their daughter Lupe was a concert pianist who played with the Jalapa Symphony Orchestra. I often accompanied her to concerts. The family took us to sites of Mayan and Aztec ruins and to the cities of México, Puebla and Veracruz. One day, the entire extended family took Dennis, Jeff and me to a beach north of Veracruz. We swam and played games followed by a tasty lunch served by *las señoras* (the ladies).

Unintentionally, I gave the family some gray hairs the first week in their care. A group of us hiked up El Cofre Mountain. We became separated when a local boy took me to get a drink of spring water. To make a long story short, the others thought I had already gone down to the village where we originally started our climb and returned to Jalapa. In the meantime, I waited at the designated rendezvous point until it was nearly dark, then ran frantically down the mountain. Once I reached the road unscathed, a car came by. The driver said, "You must be the boy lost on the mountain." He drove me to the police station. The López family was there along with an armed search team that had been assembled to find me. They were relieved, to say the least, when I stepped out of the car. There were no more hair-raising incidents.

30

At the end of our program, Miguel López, the eldest son, drove us to Acapulco. For one week, we bathed in the sun, toured Acapulco Bay by ship, saw the famous cliff divers at La Quebrada and we three males had our first introduction to a red-light district.

Dennis, Cathy, David & Jeff
Acapulco, México – 1965

Janet Washburn, a first runner up to Miss Minnesota, participated in that program. The following spring break we went to Fort Lauderdale. My brother Jim loaned us his station wagon. In exchange, Janet gave him her Metropolitan. John Bolz, a classmate, drove down with us. We stayed with his grandparents in Lauderdale-By-The-Sea. His grandmother introduced me to the wonderful delicacy escargot. They took us to Key West, a quiet little village in the 1960s — before the arrival of cruise ships. One afternoon, John fell asleep on the beach and suffered a terrible sunburn. His father, a physician, advised him to fly home.

While we were basking in sunny Florida, a blizzard struck Minnesota. We returned to more than a foot of fresh snow and huge drifts. Jim, meanwhile, negotiated Minneapolis streets in Janet's little car. It was so small that when stuck in a snowbank, people helped lift it out!

John was a ski instructor at Sugar Hills Lodge in Grand Rapids, Minnesota. Several times, I went with him to the slopes and, with his coaching, became a good skier. Our accommodations were free because we stayed at his parents' home that was located close to the lodge.

The Minnesota Twins played the Los Angeles Dodgers in the World Series when I attended the U of M. Dorothy Reardon, head cook at Pioneer Hall, sold me two extra tickets she had obtained. Jim accompanied me to a game in the old Metropolitan Stadium. The Twins won that game but lost the series in the 7th game.

Jim reported to the U.S. Coast Guard Academy in New London, Connecticut, in the summer of 1966, to accept a position as an instructor. I traveled with him in his Rambler wagon across Canada to New England. We took our time, driving only during daylight hours and camped in a tent at night. The highways took us past the Great Lakes and the Saint Lawrence Seaway, through the New York State Adirondacks and to Boston and Plymouth, Massachusetts. At the Academy, I enjoyed two days to see the immaculate campus before returning to Minneapolis from Bradley (Hartford) Airport. That was a memorable trip.

My last year at the U of M, I lived off-campus with Bill Schurman and Dick Schwartz. We rented a downstairs apartment about a mile from campus. Our landlords lived upstairs. During the winter, Bill and I shoveled the snow from their driveway and sidewalk. In appreciation, our landlady knitted me a beautiful cable-stitched sweater and often washed our laundry. Dick often came home from the dental school reeking of formaldehyde from his anatomy course. Bill worked for Independent Millworks a few blocks away. He dated my sister Sue and they were married in 1967, shortly before I graduated. Bill had an easy-going disposition that helped me maintain my sanity. He loaned me his truck when I student-taught at Minneapolis Roosevelt High. My second teaching assignment took place on-campus at University High School.

During winter quarter I came down with mononucleosis, strep throat and hepatitis that forced me to drop out of school and recuperate at home. I remembered little of the ten days in the hospital, nor a two-hour ride from Minneapolis to Sauk Centre after being discharged (a bed was made in Jim's station wagon). Mother helped tremendously — a lot of tender loving care — with my recovery. When not sleeping, I read novels, including James A. Michener's *Hawaii.* Because I had progressed well in my subjects, only two instructors required me to take final exams.

In June 1967, I graduated from the University of Minnesota with a Bachelor of Science in Spanish Secondary Education. I also received a Minnesota Teaching Certificate. Memorial Stadium provided the venue for the huge ceremony of more than 10,000 graduates. Good weather made for a pleasant evening for the graduates and guests. Following the ceremony, the Petersons celebrated at Jim and Mary's house in Saint Paul.

Chapter 6

THE U.S. PEACE CORPS

In July 1967, shortly after graduating from the University of Minnesota, I joined the U.S. Peace Corps as a volunteer assigned to *la República de Panamá.* In addition to seeking adventure, it seemed like an outstanding opportunity to increase my knowledge of Spanish and to contribute something positive to the world. Ultimately, my goal was to attend graduate school and somehow incorporate the Spanish language and culture into my future. The Peace Corps also served as a temporary deferment from the Selective Service System, although I was aware that military service might be required due to the Vietnam debacle. I made many loving friends and memories while associated with that organization and became a better person as a result of my service.

(Note that references to Panamá in the following text may refer to the city or country. Ciudad Panamá is used at times to indicate the city.)

The Peace Corps served Panamá from 1963 until 1971, disbanding during the dictatorship of Manuel Noriega and returning twenty years later in 1991. Most information for this chapter came from a journal that I maintained during my two-year tour of duty. A "Description of Peace Corps Volunteer Service," included in the Addendum, summarizes my role as a volunteer in *Panamá.*

I joined 116 candidates in Philadelphia for orientation and physicals. We became Panama Group 14. Three days later, we flew on Eastern Airlines to San Juan, Puerto Rico for a three-month training program at Camp Crozier. Jack Vaughn, Director of the U.S. Peace Corps, came to the camp to welcome us.

Camp Crozier was located on the northern coast in a rain forest near the village of Rio Abajo. Our primitive living quarters — toilets and running water were outside — consisted of rows of bunk beds in army barracks called *casetas,* each with its own name. Mine was named *Caseta Arena.* We had a co-op store of which I was elected president. Carol Ritter and I managed the store and, when necessary, went to Arecibo for supplies: cigarettes, candy, toiletries, et cetera. Training was intensive with Sunday the only day without organized classes or seminars. Nevertheless, most filled part of that day studying.

David – Camp Crozier – Puerto Rico – July 1967

35

After two months of culture and language training, a small group was selected to participate in a pilot program to work in urban Panamá. Those of us in the pilot program had one week free before we reported to Panamá. Steve and Sally Fee, Bob Hayes and I flew to Saint Thomas, U.S. Virgin Islands. It offered a good respite from the previous weeks of training. We rented a car to explore the island. We were unable to find a place to stay on our last night, graciously, the U.S. Coast Guard station provided accommodations.

Upon our arrival in Panamá, we were housed at the *Hotel Colonial* in the historic district of *Casco Viejo* (Old Quarter, settled in 1673) until we obtained our own living quarters. All except Bob Hayes were assigned to Panamá. Bob was assigned to the city of Colón. Much of our free time, for the most part in the evenings, was on the roof that overlooked the Bay of Panamá. It provided a great vantage point to watch parades that passed by below, including the Independence Day parade on November 03. Eventually, I shared an apartment with Gene Niewoehner, a volunteer in Group 13. Our apartment was above a grocery store in Pueblo Nuevo, about a half-hour bus ride to the city center.

Nine of us were assigned to an urban project that presented many difficulties from the beginning. There was considerable frustration, as nearly one month was devoted to indoctrination and poorly planned training. Dan Edwards, an urban representative (staff member), worked behind the scenes to find another position for me. Of nine volunteers that started with that project, only two remained. Their backgrounds were better suited for the organization: an attorney and an urban planner.

My new assignment was with the psychological testing department at *el Instituto para la Formación y Aprovechamiento de Recursos Humanos* (IFARHU), a vocational training center near Tocumen International Airport. Alejandro "Alex" Cantón, a Panamanian psychologist, was the department's director. Dr. Cantón received his bachelor's degree from San Jose State University in California and a doctorate from the University of Madrid.

We administered a Spanish version of the General Aptitude Test Battery to every applicant. The tests helped determine in what course or program the candidate was qualified to participate. There were courses in carpentry, electronics, masonry and welding, for example. We tested applicants in the cities of Colón, David, Panamá and Santiago. After several months, I was given the title of Occupational Counselor with added responsibilities, but I remained a member of the psychology department. I now interviewed each person applying to the Institute. My association with IFARHU was gratifying. I left Panamá knowing that I made a positive contribution to the organization and to the Republic. The Institute continues to operate today.

David with co-workers Dalaida, Carolina & Alex
IFARHU – Panamá – 1968

IFARHU provided a wonderful opportunity. The Center invited me to accompany Dr. Cantón to visit a similar program in Santiago, Chile and attend a psychology conference in Montevideo, Uruguay. The Peace Corps and IFARHU partially funded the trip.

When our meetings concluded in Montevideo, I trekked through Argentina, Bolivia and Perú. That trip was too extensive to document here except for a fascinating boat trip across Lake Titicaca — the highest navigable lake in the world — from Bolivia to Perú and a hike to Machu Picchu, Perú. The latter was the most inspiring place I have experienced. On that hike, I met two women who were volunteers with a Canadian organization equivalent to the U.S. Peace Corps. The three of us slept overnight in the Incan ruins. In the morning, we climbed Huaynu Picchu, situated high above Machu Picchu. The peak offered a spectacular view of the ancient city and the Urubamba River valley. We stood speechless as we gazed at the site below. In the Cuzco area, we saw more ruins and witnessed indigenous Quechua ceremonies. My South American adventure ended in Lima, Perú in April of 1969.

The Peace Corps years were among the most significant of my life. In addition to developing a stronger identification with Latin American culture, it was a time of introspection. I befriended Panamanians, Peace Corps volunteers (PCVs) and people from the Canal Zone (C.Z.). Alex and Emita Cantón became lifetime friends. I was a frequent guest in their home and associated with Alex's siblings and his mother, Cecelia. I devoured the Panamanian food: fresh fruit, abundant seafood (ceviche was a favorite), rice and a variety of legumes. Panamanians told me that I was *más panameño que gringo* (more Panamanian than North American)! A very nice compliment.

Some *amigos panameños* invited me to *Carnavales* in Las Tablas in the province of Los Santos. The weekend was filled with eating, street dancing and revelry. The Carnival — Mardi Gras Panama-style — is a massive celebration lasting many consecutive days preceding *Cuaresma* (Lent). Native costumes are worn by many of the participants. The *pollera,* the typical celebration dress of women worn particularly at formal events, is white with colorful flowers embroidered on it, often taking one year to make. The woman's head is decorated with a *tembleque panameño* (an ornament made of beads). Men wear the simpler attire of the *montuno* (native peasant), which consists of white trousers, a *panabrisa* (a loose white shirt worn outside the trousers) and a Panama hat (white with an upturned brim and wide band).

On another weekend, *panameños* invited me to witness the construction of *Casa de Manuel F. Zárate,* a folklore museum in Guararé, also in Los Santos Province. The structure was made of wood and *embarra* (adobe). The *embarra* was made from scratch right in front of the structure. Rows of men — with arms locked — tramped in their bare feet through mud and straw until it reached the desired consistency. They carried masses of the mixture on their shoulders to men who applied it to the framework. It was a big event with typical food cooked in huge caldrons and women and men dressed in native costumes.

Panamá is a fascinating country. Its three major cities are Colón (on the Atlantic coast), Panamá (on the Pacific coast) — each at one end of the Panama Canal — and David, located not far from the border of Costa Rica. Its people are of many origins: indigenous people, mestizos, Asians, Indians (from the sub-continent), blacks of African descent from the West Indies and Jamaica (they originally came to help build the Panama Canal and were hired because of their knowledge of English) and Europeans. Spanish is the national language but most everyone speaks English, as well. Panamanians are attractive, genuine, happy and festive.

The country has a diverse topography and climate, with the unique geographical anomaly of an isthmus — between the Atlantic and Pacific Oceans — that connects the two Americas. The Darién, alleged to be the densest jungle in the world and teeming with wildlife, borders Colombia. In Chiriquí Province, adjacent to the Costa Rican border, are mountains with cold streams. The immense landform of Barú, an extinct volcano reaching a height of more than 11,400 feet, is the highest mountain in Panamá. That mountain province is known for white-water rafting. Both coasts are bathed with warm ocean waters that are ideal for swimming and fishing. Panamá has many pristine beaches, including Santa Clara, on the Pacific coast. Fresh fruit is abundant everywhere, coffee is a major product and, surprisingly, cattle are numerous in western provinces. There are virtually only two seasons: winter

David Peterson

(November through January or February) and summer — or more accurately, dry and rainy, respectively.

The *Canal de Panamá* (Panama Canal) is approximately 50 miles long connecting the Pacific and Atlantic Oceans. When I lived in Panamá it was operated by the Panama Canal Company, an American enterprise. The U.S. Canal Zone, a swath of land fifty-miles long by ten-miles wide — off-limits to most Panamanians — essentially cut Panamá in half. It was not until 1962, with the completion of the *Puente de las Américas* (Bridge of the Americas), that a road bridge connected the eastern part of the country to the west. Until that time, barges and ferries were used. (The Canal continued to be operated by the United States until January 01, 2000 when it reverted to the control of the Republic of Panamá. It continues to be very important for shipping and tourism.)

The Zone had an appearance of a large southern plantation. We, as volunteers with U.S. passports, went there for "R and R." Summit Gardens had picnic areas and a zoo containing only native species. More importantly, the Tivoli Hotel offered cocktails and meals at an affordable price. I witnessed The *U.S.S. New Jersey* transit the canal en route to Vietnam in 1968, creating an extraordinary sight. The huge battleship was so wide that only inches remained between ship and concrete walls.

One afternoon, C.Z. friends took me to Veracruz Beach. Swimming along a sandbar, I encountered a sting ray. The large winged monster was better armed than I and stung me with its sharp barb. My leg quickly swelled from the venom. The next two days I was in the care of Gorgas Hospital staff. There were other PCVs in Panamá that did not fare as well. At least one died from malaria and another was hospitalized with a mysterious infection.

On October 11, 1968, a military *coup d'état* took place. *La Guardia Nacional de Panamá* (The National Police Force of Panamá) overthrew the constitutional government of the recently elected President Arnulfo Árias who was only in office eleven days. President Árias was ousted when he tried to order Lieutenant Colonel Omar Torrijos to a foreign post. Most Panamanians opposed the coup and ensuing *junta* that led to rioting across the country. In front of my apartment, people were shot and cars were overturned and burned. *La Guardia Nacional* used brutal force to quickly take control of the country. PCVs were advised to stay at home and were given preliminary evacuation procedures. Evacuation did not come to pass. However, Omar Torrijos remained the Commander of the National Guard and the *de facto* dictator of Panamá from 1968 to 1981. (Panamá later returned to a stable democracy.)

Those were turbulent years in the United States too with the assassinations of Martin Luther King Jr. and Robert Kennedy, plus the effects of the Vietnam War. At least two volunteers were drafted while serving in Panamá, including my pal Mike DeRienzo. Considering we were so far removed from the States, it was difficult to comprehend the events taking place "back home."

Living in Ciudad Panamá afforded me the flexibility to explore the country and visit fellow PCVs at their sites. Volunteers were assigned to urban, rural or remote areas. Because the cost of living in the capital was high, urban volunteers barely survived on their subsistence levels. However, the city did have some advantages: restaurants, movie theaters, good transportation, news media and more contact with other volunteers.

Carol Ritter (also based in the city) and I traveled together throughout the country. We had the advantage of working "9 to 5" Monday through Friday. Three memorable places we visited were the archipelago of San Blas to see Jim Linscott and Sandy Podzus, the mountain village of Boquete in the Costa Rican foothills and the Darién jungle to see Jan and Maggie Dobbs.

San Blas, home to the native Kuna (Guna), is a group of islands located in the Kuna Yala District in the northeast of Panama facing the Caribbean Sea. Carol, Jim, Sandy and I went by *cayuco* (a vessel carved from the trunk of a tree, a dugout), propelled by an outboard Evinrude, to several different islands, sleeping in hammocks and cooking our meals over a fire on uninhabited islands. We visited Kuna villages and

41

purchased *molas* (layers of fabric sewn together to make beautiful designs that form part of a woman's blouse).

Jim and Sandy joined Carol and me on a four-day getaway to Boquete in Chiriquí Province, a seven-hour drive from Ciudad Panamá. PC Deputy Director Kathy Doyle kindly loaned us her car. Located in a mountain valley with fresh air and abundant streams, Boquete had the appearance of a Swiss village. It was the only time that I recall the need to wear a sweater in Panamá.

On March 30, 1968, Carol and I flew to the Darien to visit Jan and Maggie. Their little village had a grass runway about a mile from their dwelling. The Dobbs lived in a thatched hut built on stilts in an isolated area. They had a pet monkey, an ocelot and a deer and raised chickens. One evening, we "cruised" the river in Jan's dugout watching wildlife, especially alligators, on shore and in water, at times only their eyes were visible slightly above the water line. I acquired a little *perico* (a small parrot with mostly green feathers) on April Fool's Day and named him *Tonto* ("Fool"). Tonto soon learned to say his name plus other words, in Spanish. I gave my little feathered friend to Víctor, a neighbor boy, when I moved from Pueblo Nuevo to the barrio of Parque Lefevre.

Jim stayed with me whenever he came to Panamá. It gave us a chance to bond and share experiences. More importantly, he avoided hotel expenses. Any money saved could be used for dining out, a movie or travel.

Violet LaMont, a widow and volunteer in Group 14, joined the Peace Corps at age 54, my parents' age, at the time. She worked in the PC office in an administrative capacity and joined Carol and me on a few of our escapades. Our last year in Panamá, Violet and I rented rooms from Dor Campbell, our Jamaican landlady. Living in Parque Lefevre with Dor was a positive experience. She introduced us to her relatives and friends and included us when they came to visit. Dor was a good cook who regularly asked us to join her for dinner. Violet and I willingly shared in the household expenses. We were fortunate to have the opportunity to live in a private home, especially one with a gracious landlady. Years later, I visited Violet in Portland, Oregon, when I worked for Braniff International Airways.

A favorite retreat involved an escape to Taboga, an island 12 nautical miles from Ciudad Panamá reached in one hour by launch. The small island had a quaint village with narrow streets that were adorned with flowers. A plaza contained one of the oldest churches in the hemisphere. Homes of wealthy Panamanians dotted the island. It had a beautiful natural harbor filled with yachts from around the world. It was especially popular with volunteers from rural areas to relax in the sun, swim and snorkel in the crystal-clear water.

On a launch returning from a day trip to Taboga, I met a vice president of Phillips Petroleum and an officer of the Latin American division of a major publishing company. They invited me to meet them for dinner later that evening. During the rest of my service, I joined them when they were in the country.

Aunt Ethel and Uncle Orvylle Johnson wrote to me that they had friends working for the Panama Canal Company. Because I felt obligated to "establish" myself in Panamá, I did not immediately try to get in touch with them. Several months later, I contacted Al and Cecelia Waldorf in the Canal Zone. As their guest, I went to yacht clubs and other privileged venues. I joined them for a cookout and a dance. Cecilia and I danced all evening. Al and I celebrated our November birthdays together at the Tivoli Hotel: his was the 21st and mine the 22nd. They introduced me to a C.Z. police officer. In the months that followed, Norb and I explored many rural areas of Panamá. He often invited me to join him and other officers. Most noteworthy, I was a groomsman in his wedding held in Ancon Church in the Zone.

Mother and Dad flew to Panamá to visit, thanks to Karen's employee benefits with Braniff International. Most of our time was spent in the city environs. One evening, Deputy Director Kathy Doyle entertained us in her home. Kathy accompanied us on a boat tour of the

Panama Canal. We passed through the Miraflores Locks and the incredibly narrow Galliard Cut (also called Culebra Cut), an excavated gorge more than eight miles long across the Continental Divide.

Ship transiting the Galliard Cut – Panama Canal – 1968

A highlight was a trip to the San Blas Islands. Excitement began when the single engine aircraft landed on the small island's tiny air strip. Safely on the ground, we were met by our hosts Jim and Sandy. Sandy shared her hut with my parents. I stayed on a nearby island with Jim. The toilet, at the end of a pier several feet above the ocean, intrigued Mother. It had no plumbing, of course: just a wooden frame that provided privacy. Despite netting over her bed, Mother was concerned that a vampire bat might bite her at night.

Jim transported us in his *cayuco* to El Tigre Island inhabited by Kunas. Sandy was our guide and translator. Our return voyage had anxious moments as we encountered *agua brava* (very rough sea). Sandy and I were kept busy bailing water with coconut shells! Mother and Dad were covered with a tarpaulin that protected them from the elements. They congratulated Jim on getting us back safely.

I flew to the Bahamas to meet a university classmate in September of 1968. She and I shared an affinity for the Spanish language and Scotch whiskey. We originally planned to travel to South America, but she was unable to get a security clearance due to her position with the Defense Intelligence Agency. Special dispensation was given to me in order to meet her in Miami, as PC policy prohibited a return to the U.S. mainland during one's tour of duty. We enjoyed two wonderful weeks in the Bahamas. Our parents and PC staff heard wedding bells, however we decided to go our separate ways.

Panama Group 14 volunteers were officially discharged in August 1969, following successful completion of a two-year term. A three-day debriefing was held on Taboga Island. Testing to determine our language proficiency was included. My Foreign Service Institute certificate states: "Full professional ability in the Spanish language." I realized that I had mastered Spanish the first time I dreamed in that language, sometime during my tour in Panamá.

Following our discharge, John Overholt, a PCV in my group, traveled with me through Central America. From Guatemala City, John flew to the States. I continued to Jalapa, México to visit the López family with whom I lived during my University of Minnesota study program. They were impressed with my fluent Spanish but, nevertheless, teased me about the Panamanian accent. Over time, I made a concerted effort to pronounce words clearly and avoid the habits of coastal Spanish — as spoken in Panamá. After my Jalapa visit, I went to Mexico City to visit Eunides Pérez, a Panamanian acquaintance who studied at the University of México. While staying with Eunides, I was given the opportunity to observe rehearsals of *Los Folkoristas,* a renowned Mexican folk-singing group. From México, I flew to San Antonio, Texas, port of entry to the United States, and finally reached Minnesota.

Not long after I arrived in Minnesota, I had an embarrassing but comical incident. On a bus in Saint Paul, I shouted — *in Spanish* — to the driver, *"En la esquina, por favor."* (advising him to let me off at the next corner). That was customary on bus routes in Panamá that did not have a cord to pull or button to push to signal the driver to stop. After weird looks from passengers and communicating with the driver *in English*, I stepped off the bus only one block past my intended stop.

In 2002, five RPCVs (returned PC volunteers who have completed their tour) in my group had a reunion in Philadelphia. Carol Ritter, Pat Pit, Ginny Berson, Suzanne Wheeling and I dined at Cuba Libre restaurant and discussed how Peace Corps affected our lives. We talked about our maladies, daily malaria pills, required injections, colorful buses and their haphazard service, prevalence of marijuana, local communities with which we were involved and the military coup.

We sadly remembered the loss of our mutual friends, including Jim Linscott who died of AIDS in 1995. We were cohorts all through Peace Corps and remained in contact throughout his life. Years later, I frequently stayed with him and his wife, Margaret, in Pasadena, California. I accompanied him to his school, on one visit, to discuss the Peace Corps with his students. Jim enjoyed teaching. His premature death devastated his parents. Jim's father sent me the following letter:

Dear David,

Mrs. Linscott and I thank you very sincerely for your thoughtful letter about Jim. He had spoken often of you, your family and your visits.

It is heartwarming and comforting to hear from Jim's long-time close friends and their feelings about him. He was a very fine son and we have always been very proud of him and his dedication to teaching and to helping young people. We will miss him terribly, but do have almost 50 years of wonderful memories.

Thank you again for your kind letter. Believe me, they do help.

Sincerely,
Henry D. Linscott

In September 2005, I accepted a thirty-day assignment with the Crisis Corps (renamed Peace Corps Response) to assist with the disaster recovery effort for victims of Hurricane Katrina. Crisis Corps operated under the auspices of the U.S. Peace Corps and employed returned PC volunteers to assist in disasters worldwide. FEMA, overwhelmed by the disaster, requested the assistance of the Crisis Corps.

I made history as a member of Katrina Response Team #1, the first time Crisis Corps was deployed within the U.S. I was assigned to FEMA's Disaster Recovery Center #2 in Marksville, Louisiana, along with co-workers from Peace Corps, Homeland Security, Customs and Border Patrol and FEMA. A close relationship developed among us, particularly between Rebecca, Michael, Mitch, Jonathan and me. We endured many stressful hours. It was a rewarding experience, although mentally and physically very challenging. A "Description of Crisis Corps Volunteer Service" describes in detail my assignment plus experiences I encountered during the recovery effort in Louisiana. A copy of that Description is in the Addendum.

Mitch, David, Jonathan and Michael
Disaster Recovery Center #2, Marksville, Louisiana

I did not take part in Peace Corps activities until many years after I returned from Panamá. There were scheduling conflicts when the 25th and 40th reunions were held. I did participate in April 2006 in the Spring Send-Off Party at the Philadelphia Free Library for new applicants about to depart to their assigned countries. I attended that event with RPCV Phil Fretz who served in Sierra Leone.

The Peace Corps celebrated its 45th anniversary in Washington, D.C. in July 2006. I stayed with Rebecca Cardozo, RPCV from Thailand who was also a Katrina colleague, and attended National PC events with her. Peace Corps Panama Friends, an organization of RPCVs from Panamá, met on separate occasions. Group 14, my group that served from 1967 to1969, had the largest representation. Most had not seen each other since our departure from Panamá. One volunteer purchased property in the Azuero Peninsula of Panamá where she relocated to establish a bed and breakfast.

David and Panamanian dancer – Peace Corps Reunion
Washington, D.C. – July 2006

The arrival of the *Pájaro Jai* on the Potomac River over the Fourth of July was coordinated with the anniversary. The ninety-foot yacht made of native woods from the Darién of Panamá was a

48

magnificent sailing vessel. Rebecca shared the afternoon with me as we explored nearly every inch of the handmade boat. Group 14 RPCV Jim Brunton, the captain, took time to describe the nearly twelve-year project constructing the *Pájaro Jai*. Jim founded the Pájaro Jai Foundation.

Chapter 7

THE UNIVERSITY OF WISCONSIN

There was little downtime to spend at home when I returned from Panamá. I planned to enroll in graduate school to pursue an MBA or MA in Spanish. Dr. Rodolfo Floripe, a former University of Minnesota Spanish professor, advised me to consider the University of Wisconsin, one of the nation's premier Spanish programs. He arranged for me to meet with Bob Mulvihill, dean of the Department of Spanish and Portuguese, in Madison. I met with Mr. Mulvihill, and soon enrolled in the 1969 fall semester. Wharton, the University of Pennsylvania's business school admitted me, but its cost was too prohibitive. Who knows where that degree would have taken me?

The University of Wisconsin offered me a stipend that covered my two-year master's degree program in Latin American Literature. I worked as a project assistant under the direction of Professor Lloyd Kasten at the Medieval Spanish Seminary. Mr. Kasten was a respected medieval scholar known worldwide. Many hours, I found myself working and drinking tea with him in the seminary or in his home library. John Nitti, a PhD candidate, worked on the project with Mr. Kasten.

As a graduate student, I had continuous contact with professors and their families. I learned etiquette and social graces as their guest. Bob Mulvihill was my advisor who became a life-long confidant. Coincidentally, he served in Panamá with the FBI during World War II. That chance led to conversations regarding the politics of Panamá. I respected Professor Mack Singleton. Despite his stature as a renowned scholar in his field, I could comfortably sit in his office and chat. His

50

classes were inspirational. Tony Cardenas was my closest colleague. He received a PhD from UW and, eventually, became chairman of the Spanish Department at the University of New Mexico.

It was not long after arriving in Madison that temperatures began to drop. My blood had thinned as a result of living two years in the tropics. Layering clothing to stay warm came naturally to me. I must have looked like a little "Teletubby" when I donned my winter attire. Fortunately, a colleague picked me up every winter morning on his way to UW parking lots. From there, we could take a shuttle bus to campus. Hot toddies kept me warm at the few Badgers football games I managed to see at Camp Randall Stadium. I cannot remember ever being colder than during that first year in Wisconsin.

There were three outstanding events that affected me in Madison. During the first semester, Bob Mulvihill realized that I was suffering from culture shock. The rapid pace, along with the political unrest in the United States, was difficult to comprehend. Once aware of my apprehension and with Bob's support, I adjusted rather well.

The second was the impact of the Vietnam War. It was a time of protest, to a great extent on university campuses. UW was no exception. There were days when the National Guard used tear gas to break up disturbances. Twice, classes were cancelled due to tear gas entering air conditioning ducts. Activists blew up the UW math research building during second semester, killing an innocent researcher. The unrest brought back memories of the military coup I witnessed in Panamá.

Due to the Vietnam War, on November 05, 1969, the Selective Service System ordered me to report to Milwaukee to take an induction physical. That winter day, I wore a heavy coat and boots. Once inside, we were required to strip down to our underwear and shoes, creating a peculiar sight. Although I was found "fully acceptable for induction," fate was on my side. President Nixon signed an executive order ending conscription for those who turned twenty-five by year's end. Otherwise, yours truly would have another chapter to write, if I were still alive.

David Peterson

I received a Master of Arts in Spanish American Literature in June 1971. That summer, I remained in Madison to complete the required hours for my stipend, audited an intensive Portuguese course and worked nights as a desk clerk at the Ivy Inn Hotel. Studying Portuguese and working at the hotel to enhance my income were in preparation for a planned trip to Europe in the fall. That rather ambitious schedule would catch up to me later while traveling in Europe.

It was a whirlwind of activity when I returned to Minnesota to prepare for my journey abroad. My sister Sue accompanied me to Minneapolis to buy hiking shoes, clothes and obtain an international driver's license and student identification. We ended the day on empty stomachs at Chuck and Alice Harrison's. The evening began with gin martinis, followed by steaks Chuck cooked on the grill. When we sat down to dine, I was dizzy, nauseated and too ill to eat. Chuck carried me to a bedroom where I slept. In the excitement, I did not realize the amount I drank. To this day, I disdain gin martinis. In any event, our errands were completed successfully.

Chapter 8

A EUROPEAN ADVENTURE

In September 1971, I flew on Sabena Airlines (Belgium's flagship carrier) from JFK Airport (New York) to Brussels to start a year-long European adventure. It was an opportune time to take advantage of a life-long dream to travel leisurely through Europe. Plans included visits to cities where UW colleagues were studying or living, and to coincide with Bob and Peg Mulvihill who were overseas during Bob's sabbatical. Before long, I discovered that traveling alone — and being a gregarious person — made it easier to meet others, an advantage that proved helpful during my journey.

A young German lad sat next to me on the transatlantic flight. When he learned of my travel plans, he invited me to accompany him to Germany. Together we walked the streets of Brussels and later toured his native city of Cologne. Three days later, he drove me to Munich where a UW art history acquaintance studied. She arranged housing, for me, before we took part in *Oktoberfest*. We were amazed watching waitresses deftly carrying several steins of beer in each hand.

I continued for two long days on a train to Athens, sharing a coach compartment with a young Canadian woman. She was returning to Greece for the first time since her family moved to Canada when she was a little girl. Before contacting her relatives, she wanted time to investigate the country on her own. We explored Athens, made easy with her fluency in the language. We went to taverns where I tasted ouzo (an anise-flavored liqueur), drank the popular *retsina* and ate delicious food. We went our separate ways when she sought her relatives.

David Peterson

In Athens, at the American Express office (a place for travelers to rendezvous and retrieve correspondence), I met a young American couple bound for Istanbul, Turkey en route to Afghanistan and India. They invited me to join them. I eagerly accepted their offer, as my itinerary was flexible. Along the way we met Judy and Shirley Johnson, two sisters from New Zealand who joined us. By bus, we journeyed to the capital city of Ankara. We climbed to the top of the Citadel: its walls high above the city offered a panoramic view. We saw the Hittite collection at the archeological museum. Dominating the Ankara skyline was the Anıtkabir grand mausoleum, the memorial tomb of Mustafa Kemal Atatürk, founder of modern Turkey. It was an imposing monument situated on the highest point of the city.

We continued to Trabzon, on the Black Sea, only a short distance from Russia. In Trabzon, we swam in the Sea, and at a local bakery ate delicious bread baked with cheese served hot and smothered in butter. The Kiwis and I sailed to Istanbul aboard the *M/VEGE* of the Turkish Maritime Lines. From Istanbul, we took a train to Plovdiv and Sophia, Bulgaria en route to Zagreb, Croatia (part of Yugoslavia in the 1970s). Plovdiv had unusual but appealing architecture. We had planned to spend a few days in Bulgaria. Regrettably, we found the residents and city very austere, so we continued to Zagreb. After two days in Zagreb, the women departed for Austria. Months later, I would join them in Oxford, England where they had a flat. I stayed a week in Zagreb with former students from UW, then went to Dubrovnik to meet the Mulvihills.

I arrived in Dubrovnik a few days before Bob and Peg. Walking along the ancient city walls, I met a nurse from San Francisco. Following a brief introduction, she invited me to share a joint, a bottle of wine and bread. We watched the sun disappear below the horizon on the Adriatic Sea and stayed in a bed and breakfast. The second morning, while we were enjoying our coffee on the patio, a deep bass voice from above asked, "Is that David Peterson down there?" By chance, the Mulvihills were upstairs in the same inn! The four of us enjoyed more days in that beautiful medieval city before my "friend" returned to San Francisco.

The Mulvihills proposed to pay my expenses if I agreed to drive. From Dubrovnik, I chauffeured the car through Yugoslavia to Italy on winding roads along the Adriatic coast. I noted in my journal that crossing the border from Yugoslavia into Italy was like night and day: technology, organization and roads were superior, and people were smiling, unlike the grim faces of the Yugoslavs. Those were days of the Iron Curtain.

The month of November, we toured Venice, Ravenna, Perugia, Assisi, Florence, Sienna, Pisa and Rome. Venice was unique with its canals instead of paved streets. It was a pleasure not to see or hear cars. Transportation was by *valporetto* (large canal boats), water taxis or gondola. *Tratorrias* and pastry shops were plentiful where one could sit down to rest with a sweet or beverage. The Palazzo Ducale off San Marco Piazza was a magnificent building with its art collection, including Tintoretto's painting *Paradise,* the world's largest oil painting.

Two weeks hardly sufficed to see the splendor of Florence. The statue of *David* at the Accademia di Belle Arti provoked in me an overwhelming feeling of reverence. The Gallerie Degli Uffizi necessitated at least two days to absorb its Italian Renaissance art collection. I was amazed by the acoustics of the Duomo and Baptistry. Every corner of *Firenze* offered something for the eye. Aside from art, the city had great clothing bargains. I purchased two sweaters.

Burning the candle at both ends in Madison, prior to my trip to Europe, finally caught up to me in Florence. I was completely run down. Bob contacted the American consulate to have a doctor see me at the inn where we were staying. He prescribed iron supplements plus other medication to relieve my fatigue and cough. I soon bounced back to continue our journey to *Roma.*

The Italian capital was packed with things to see, including the Coliseum and Pantheon. The Vatican, despite its opulence, required a visit to view its immense art collection. One could only stare up in awe at

Michelangelo's ceiling in the Sistine Chapel to absorb perhaps the greatest work of art ever painted, certainly one of the most difficult.

We managed a side trip to Pisa where I climbed the famous leaning tower that I learned of as a child. In Italy, I attempted to climb almost every church or city tower that I encountered.

When a week in Rome passed, I flew to Portugal to stay with John and Manuela Nitti. (John and I worked together in the UW Spanish Department.) Manuela hailed from Colares, a small community west of Lisbon. She and John were living with her parents while he studied in preparation for his PhD. I saw much of the fascinating Portuguese culture, with them. They took me to dine in local restaurants and to hear *fado* (Portuguese folk music) in nightclubs. When not with the Nittis, I wandered the countryside on any available mode of transportation.

I met Tim Clark in Lisbon in December 1971. Together, we admired the impressive collection of royal carriages at the coach museum and spent hours in the planetarium and Portuguese naval museum. The beautiful Jerónimos Monastery — one of the finest examples of Manueline architecture — was another place we admired. Lisbon is known for its unusual Manueline architecture and colorful *azulejo* (a ceramic tile attached to facades of buildings). We explored the Moorish castle in Sintra, a short distance from the city. We reconnected in the States and have remained friends. For a while, we both lived in Dallas at the same time. It has been interesting comparing Tim's annual Christmas photos of him and his wife Sandy and daughter Elisa.

In Lisbon, I also met Jim Bucko who was recently discharged from the U.S. Navy. At first, he thought I was a local street vendor. Perhaps my beard and European clothes confused him. Delightfully, introductions resulted in a positive connection which led to many interesting experiences. On Christmas Day, we set out for Spain, by train, making it to Beja, Portugal. All businesses were closed because of the holiday. With assistance of the local police, we found a *pensión*. Two officers paid for our meal and wine at a family restaurant. We shared Christmas Eve in a bar with the delightful company of Portuguese.

From Beja, we hitched a ride with a group of Australians to Rota, Spain. Jim had buddies at the Navy base in Rota. In the ensuing months, their apartment in view of the Atlantic Ocean would become our home. The sailors were extremely accommodating. On base, we could eat and see a movie for free! D.D. Brown drove us to nearby sites. Rota served as our headquarters while we discovered other parts of southern Spain and Morocco. Curiously, our travels closely mirrored those in Michener's novel *The Drifters*.

Crossing the Mediterranean Sea on a ferry from Algeciras, Spain to Africa, Jim and I met Cris LeGassey who became a traveling companion. The port of Algeciras was adjacent to Gibraltar, but we were unable to visit "The Rock" because travel from Spain to Gibraltar was not permitted. However, our ferry passed within spitting distance of the British Territory. Once on Moroccan soil, we traveled, by bus and train — including the famous Marrakech Express — from the port of Tangiers to Casablanca, Rabat, Marrakech, Agadir, Fez, McNes and Ceuta. The city of Fez faced the Atlas Mountains. It was divided into three sections: Arabian, Jewish and the modern European sector. The Medina of Fez (a World Heritage Site) is surrounded by massive walls and gates.

The most intriguing Moroccan city was Marrakech. We extended our stay for a week due to its fascination. A terrace overlooked the plaza from where we watched the activity below. The medina was full of vendors selling goods of all kinds, including the "hash cookie man." There were watermen — always a threesome — in colorful red costumes selling water, dancers and snake charmers. The atmosphere was intoxicating. We rode camels for the first time. The Kasbah bustled with activity, and the dyers market was incredibly colorful with its brightly colored yarn hanging out to dry. At night, the plaza transformed into a food bazaar. We ate our meals in tents that served delicious food. It was not necessarily sanitary, as we ate off plates that were merely rinsed off in barrels of water before they served us. None of us was apparently any worse off eating with the locals.

David and Jim – Marrakech, Morocco – 1972

As we were making our "escape" from Morocco at the port of Ceuta, Jim and I realized that we had left behind, in a restaurant, bags containing our black capes that we had so diligently bargained for in the Souks. We hired a cab to retrieve them, barely returning in time to catch a ferry to Spain. Eventually, I donated my cape to a local theatre company.

Karen flew to Malaga, Spain to join me during the month of February. We drove to Torremolinos in D.D. Brown's Volkswagen and relaxed for two days at the Marbella Hilton on the shores of the Mediterranean. In order for Karen to experience the intrigue of Morocco, we left the VW at the port of Algeciras, then took a ferry to Tangiers. The hotel owner recognized me from the previous trip with Jim. Although a Moroccan, she spoke fluent Spanish, in addition to Arabic and French, so we had no difficulty communicating. She directed us to restaurants and places to shop. One evening, she dressed Karen in traditional Arab clothing, including a *burka* and *hijab,* and me in a caftan and fez.

In Spain, on our way to Granada and Córdoba, we drove through mountains past tiny whitewashed villages and olive groves. Every mountaintop had an imposing Moorish tower, castle or cathedral that was visible for miles. We walked through marvelous buildings and gardens in those cities built by Moors. The Alhambra in Granada was an amazing sight with its fountains and gardens. The Alcázar in Córdoba, considered the best-preserved Moorish labyrinth of arched columns in the world, was fascinating. Regrettably, *los católicos* (Christians) built a huge cathedral right in the middle, destroying much of it. Before Karen departed from *Sevilla*, she "loaned" me money that enabled me to extend my stay in Europe.

In Madrid, Jim and I contacted Cris, our traveling companion in Morocco. Manuel, her attractive *madrileño*, found us an inexpensive place to stay. Manuel and his pals invited us to partake in some traditional Spanish customs, including *ir de mesones* (going from bar to bar while groups of university students try to "outsing" each other).

We walked around Madrid taking in as many sites as possible. The Prado Museum occupied two days of our time, still we only scratched its surface. We thoroughly viewed my favorite 17th century painting *Las meninas* (*Maids of Honor*) by Diego Velázquez. It has been considered one of the most admired group portraits — of that period — of little Princess Margarita with her attendants. In the Plaza Santa Ana, La Cervecería Alemana continued to be a favorite place to imbibe. Ernest Hemingway favored it too and allegedly wrote some of his novels there. It was a cozy place to relax in a little corner of Spain.

Cris remained in Madrid; Jim went to Germany; and I set off for Barcelona. On Easter Sunday, I watched Catalonians perform traditional folk dances in church courtyards. At times, there was a single circle that developed into two or three intermingled circles. Tulips and other plants were in full bloom in Montjuich Park, a sprawling landscape overlooking the Mediterranean Sea. It was an ideal time to be in Barcelona. The culture, friendly people, cuisine and my familiarity with the vernacular reinforced my feelings that Spain was my favorite country.

Eventually, I made it to England and stayed in London with Peace Corps friends Gayle and Michael Lang. Michael was studying economics at a London university. The most interesting time with them included an extensive tour of Windsor Castle.

After a few days, I went to Oxford to rejoin my Kiwi friends. Their flat was in easy walking distance to the city center. Judy worked at a hospital and Shirley worked at the Lamb and Flag, a typical English pub. I became enamored with Oxford where I listened to organ and choral music in the chapels at various universities. New College, with its beautiful stained-glass windows, most impressed me. We frequently punted (used a pole to push a small boat) on the Thames River, a popular pastime of Oxford.

Shirley and I thumbed our way across England to Wales, first in a lorry, then a Jaguar. We ferried from Fishguard, Wales to Ballygeary, Ireland where we hired a car. We stayed with the McMahons — Shirley's distant relatives — in Liscanor, a little fishing village a short distance from the Cliffs of Moer on the western coast in County Clare. The cliffs were spectacular but dangerous due to high winds coupled with pounding Atlantic surf. During our stay in Liscanor, the *Apollo 16* space craft was circling the globe. We watched it splash down on television in a local smokey pub that was heated by peat.

We continued our travels north up the coast, sleeping in youth hostels along the way. We slept in two converted coast guard stations, one in Galway and another in Donegal. Our last stop in Ireland was Clonmany, the most northern point on the west coast. From there we went inland, crossing into Northern Ireland.

In the village of Eniskillen we caused quite a stir. We found a convenient place to park our car. When we returned, the police had barricaded the street and roped off the car. We were unaware that vehicles could not be left unattended unless parked in designated areas, due to terrorism. The police interrogated us, determined that our car was not a bomb threat, then eagerly — and much relieved — sent us on our way. The rest of our trip was uneventful except for close encounters with cattle or sheep crossing the narrow roads.

Europe would soon be left behind as I found my way back to Brussels to board a Sabena flight to New York. Bob Hayes, an RPCV who served with me in Panamá, met me at JFK airport. We drove directly to his City Island flat. In the days that followed, we saw the rock opera *Tommy* by The Who, and Bob gave me an excellent tour of New York.

Slowly, I began to work a circuitous way back to Minnesota. I took a train from New York to Philadelphia to pay a visit with Suzanne and Paul Wheeling, Panama RPCVs. Suzanne trimmed my beard and gave me a long overdue haircut. Philadelphia positively impressed me, especially, after hearing its praises from the Wheelings. Little did I know that Philly would one day be my home.

I hitchhiked from Philly to Wisconsin with multiple stops in between. In State College, Pennsylvania, I visited Gerry and Rita Gau, U of M classmates; in Chicago, I stayed with Diane Erickson, a U of M classmate; in Madison, Wisconsin, I stayed with Tony and Diane Cardenas; and finally, I reached Eau Claire, Wisconsin where Dick and Ellen Schwartz lived. Dick, a DDS, gave me dental care. A few days later, they drove me to Sauk Centre. Conveniently, they had a summer cabin on nearby Birch Lake.

Chapter 9

LIVING IN QUEENS

Jim Bucko and I decided to live in New York City. His Navy pals had an apartment in Forest Hills, Queens Borough and invited us to stay with them. In the summer of 1972, Jim drove from his mother's home in Madison, Wisconsin to Sauk Centre. All of our belongings fit in his VW Beetle. We drove from Minnesota to New York to start a new life in apartment 5L. The apartment number was significant because a Chinese restaurant only managed to successfully deliver our food when we said, "5R, as in Rondon." Peter, Earl, Jim and I shared that crowded apartment. I slept on a mattress in the living room or used an empty bed when a roommate was gone.

A friend of Earl's worked at the JFK Airport Hilton and arranged an interview for me. The manager hired me at once. I moved to Rockaway Boulevard to be closer to the hotel. I worked as a desk clerk, front office manager and, lastly, credit manager. The Hilton was a great place to meet people. Billy Joel was a guest the night a telegram advised him that "Piano Man" had sold one million records. I presented him with the telegram and with a vigorous handshake. Elvis Presley stayed there when he performed at Nassau County Coliseum, but we only saw glimpses of him due to his security staff. Braniff flight attendants had crew rooms there, some of whom were acquaintances of my sister Karen. Several horsemen rented monthly rooms and gave hotel employees free entrance passes to Aqueduct and Belmont racetracks

A Mind of his Own

The Hilton was a promiscuous place. I dated several employees, including a waitress, bar maid, hostess and night clerk. The hostess and I frequented Jones Beach, visited hotel associates on Long Island and attended concerts and other events in the metropolitan area. We traveled in her MGB convertible around New York State, along the Mohawk trail in Massachusetts and visited the Wilsons in Athol. We flew to Panamá to visit Alex and Emita Cantón.

Joe Steiniger, a restaurant manager next door at Howard Johnson's, and I became buddies. He was a friend of Peter and Earl and a frequent visitor to 5L. We devoted many evenings to dining in Manhattan's Chinatown. Because Joe was a frequent patron of one restaurant, the staff discretely set aside a bottle of Scotch in the kitchen, for him. I enjoyed listening to him sing and play the guitar. Joe moved to Poughkeepsie and became my financial advisor. His smile and sincerity were qualities that made him a successful businessman. There was one early — unsuccessful — transaction he told me to use as a dart board! There have been no complaints since.

New York presented an opportunity to experience culture more than any other city in the world. Central Park was a favorite place. I attended concerts there by the New York Philharmonic and saw Simon and Garfunkel perform there. I strolled through the zoo, sat by the lake and contemplated at a favorite resting place dedicated to Lewis Carroll. I became quite enamored with the bronze statue of the *Mad Hatter* with its inscription about Tweedledum and Tweedledee that I memorized:

> *"Tweedledum and Tweedledee*
> *Agreed to have a battle;*
> *For Tweedledum said Tweedledee*
> *Had spoiled his nice new rattle.*
>
> *Just then flew down a monstrous crow,*
> *As black as a tar-barrel;*
> *Which frightened both the heroes so,*
> *They quite forgot their quarrel!"*

David Peterson

Jim and I thoroughly enjoyed our sojourn in New York City. Central Park was also one of his favorite places too. One evening, while driving Jim's Volkswagen Beetle, a prized possession that he brought over from Germany, I was involved in a hit-and-run accident on the Van Wyck Expressway. While at work, Jim claimed he had a premonition that something had happened to me. He photographed me posed in front of the smashed VW — a total loss — in a lot to where it had been towed.

Subsequently, we drove his *new* Fiat to Florida, pausing to see Cypress Gardens and Disney World. Our return trip routed us through the picturesque Blue Ridge Mountains with a stop at Monticello, the home and architectural masterpiece of Thomas Jefferson. Monticello and the University of Virginia — also designed by Jefferson — are UNESCO World Heritage Sites. Gettysburg and Washington, D.C. were other places we saw. Jim moved to Virginia to take advantage of an employment opportunity, but our friendship continued. Serendipity brought us together years later in Florida where he owned a home near Jim and Gail.

Karen came to New York several times, twice, with Mother and Dad. The first time, we toured the city, went to Radio City Music Hall and rode the Circle Line (a sightseeing cruise that completely circumnavigated Manhattan). We drove the length of Long Island all the way to Montauk Point. On another visit, we four drove from New York to Athol, Massachusetts to call upon my cousin Marilyn and her husband, Hal. Uncle Carol and Aunt Tib were there in anticipation of a trip to Nova Scotia with my parents.

Chapter 10

BRANIFF INTERNATIONAL AIRWAYS

Karen was hired as a "hostess" by Braniff International Airways (BI) in 1960. Because I was spending hard-earned money, mostly on travel and entertainment, we agreed that airline employment could offer me the same, plus a salary. I accepted a flight attendant position with Braniff in May 1976 and flew until 1982 when the company closed.

Braniff was known worldwide as a result of its "flying colors" and excellent service. It was the only airline named after a specific person, its founder, Thomas Braniff. Harding Lawrence, BI's president in the 1970s, teamed up with Mary Wells and her advertising company to make a bold statement for the carrier. Not only was it the first airline to paint the entire fuselage of its aircraft, it was done in solid metallic colors such as beige, orange, yellow, green, blue and turquoise! Orange was reserved only for the 747 aircraft. The company painted one aircraft in patriotic red, white and blue, designed by Alexander Calder. It was an exciting airline, particularly, during the revolutionary time of deregulation.

The intensive flight attendant training was conducted at Braniff's headquarters in Dallas, Texas. Its emphasis consisted mostly of learning the company's various aircrafts and emergency skills, the primary responsibilities of a flight attendant. Substantial time was devoted to in-flight service. In the 1970s, first class was an elegant china service. Even tourist class had a choice of meals and beverages. Braniff was world-renowned for its superb service. Flight attendants learned to identify wine by the shape of the bottle, properly "set a table" and serve from a cart. Flying for BI, I developed a greater knowledge and taste for fine wine.

Although we flew several flights as trainees where we practiced what we learned in our classes, the bulk of our knowledge was learned on-the-job.

There was a security threat shortly after takeoff on our first 747 training flight to Honolulu. The tower mandated the flight crew to return Fat Albert — nickname of the orange Boeing 747 — to DFW (Dallas-Fort Worth Airport). The full aircraft needed more than one hour to dump fuel — to lighten the load — in order to make a safe landing. Once it was determined that no bomb was aboard and it was safe to fly, the jumbo jet took off again, *sans* all cargo, including U.S. mail. Karen's flight pattern regularly took her to Hawaii, so she arranged to meet our flight in Hawaii's warm tradition of greeting me and my classmates with leis.

When in-flight training was completed, I lived with Karen until I found a place of my own. Her apartment was at The Castilian, not far from Love Field. Residents were a diverse group, many of whom were aspiring professionals. There were elaborate parties, including an annual luau with ice sculptures, island food and music accompanied by Samoan dancers. I met Willie R Spencer and Bil Milton there. Willie R would later own a condominium near me and become a dear friend. Bil Milton helped me get acquainted with Dallas and included me in his social life. One afternoon, he stopped me at the apartment to invite me to a Neil Diamond concert in Fort Worth. Still in uniform, I quickly snatched clothes and changed in the car. Neil gave a superb concert.

Steve Guarnaschelli settled in with me at the Hud Apartments on Cedar Springs Road. Steve came from Orlando where he worked for Disney World. That clean-cut saintly appearance — typical of Disney employees — did not fool me. With his wit and amusing humor, he qualified as a good roommate. I took advantage of his contacts in Orlando and enjoyed complimentary passes at the amusement park that included behind-the-scene tours.

Because I was fluent in Spanish, I immediately obtained scheduled flight patterns instead of being placed on call as a reserve. Initially, most flights were to México and South America. It was not uncommon to be the most junior cabin crew member yet responsible for making all announcements in English and Spanish — and Portuguese, when necessary — and handling customs documentation. My first Christmas, I was the lead attendant on a charter to Rio de Janeiro that included a five-day layover, a marvelous introduction to that city.

As BI grew with deregulation, so did my seniority and a chance to fly virtually around the world. I could visit friends and see new destinations. I flew international routes and overseas charters whenever possible. Bill Holyfield and I enjoyed our first vacation in Hawaii as Braniff employees, visiting Oahu, Maui and the big island of Hawaii. On a three-day weekend in Philadelphia during the 1976 bicentennial celebration, I managed to spend time with RPCV Carol Ritter. One month, my pattern included flights to Minneapolis with a layover in New Orleans. The cabin crew and I managed to "smuggle" my younger sister on board. Sue flew with us to New Orleans and roomed with a female flight attendant. On that two-day weekend layover, we had a good time touring the Big Easy while enjoying classic Hurricane cocktails.

I opted for Seattle layovers to spend time with Cris LeGassey. Cris introduced me to Neal Robertson and Carol Davison. I shared delightful moments with those two who died prematurely, Neal of AIDS and Carol of cancer. Carol and I were accused of being obnoxious when we were together, especially, if we were a little high, had a few glasses of wine, or both, and laughed uncontrollably. She met me at SEA (Seattle Airport) when Cris was at work. With free time on our hands, we easily found a way to get into trouble. The Davisons had a cabin in a secluded place on the Hood Canal off Puget Sound, a pleasant place to unwind.

I took many excursions with Cris. We drove several times to witness the Omak Stampede in eastern Washington. On our way to Omak, we stopped to view the light show at Grand Coulee Dam on the Columbia River and hiked in Cascades National Park. Traveling south from Seattle to Crescent City, California on our way to visit her aunt Nina, we followed roads through giant redwoods. Lupine and California poppies were flowering in Mendocino County. On our return, we sampled wine at Parducci Vineyards (some of the best wine in America). Whidbey Island — accessed only by ferry — became a favorite destination, often accompanied with an overnight at the Captain Whidbey, a charming hotel and several log cabins located on a little cove. It had an excellent restaurant and bar in view of the cove. Jim Bucko coordinated a trip to Seattle that included a Whidbey Island layover with Cris, Carol and me.

I met Frank Pesce, an Air Canada customer service agent, on a flight from Tampa to Dallas in 1977. Months later, my schedule included layovers in Tampa where Frank lived and we arranged a rendezvous. It did not take long to realize that we were attracted to each other. I chose patterns with Tampa layovers and soon began to commute from there. His apartment was in walking distance to Tampa Bay where I spent sunny afternoons collecting shells and watching wildlife.

We were partners for nearly five years. It was the first gay relationship for both of us. There was no specific date or time that I accepted being gay. In retrospect, realizing it was not a choice but a fact of life was a significant step that made it easier to cope with its inherent difficulties and discrimination. Our circle of friends greatly expanded because of our type of work and Frank's cheerful disposition. Everybody liked him. Both sets of parents lovingly supported us. While his parents were living in Fort Myers, Florida, we enjoyed quality time with them. Elsie and Larry were an endearing couple. They were inseparable. Following Elsie's death, Larry could not cope with his loss and died soon after of a broken heart.

Together, we explored Florida, including Everglades National Park and Key West. Frank nearly suffered a heart attack when a huge snake crossed our path in Everglades Park. Once he recovered, we scurried off before two people came down the same narrow trail. (The whole story of what happened to Frank will be left to your imagination.) In the Tampa area, we saw Ibor City, Tarpon Springs, Busch Gardens and Saint Petersburg. Once, we ventured to Georgia to see the huge anomaly at Stone Mountain before continuing to Atlanta.

When Frank bought a new Oldsmobile, I purchased his 1976 Cutlass Supreme. We drove "Goldie" from Tampa to its new home in Texas, stopping in Mobile, Alabama to walk among the azaleas at Bellingrath Gardens, then continued down the road to New Orleans to relax for a few days.

Frank transferred to DFW and we moved into an apartment on Cedar Springs Road. His friend, Lucy Rohrer, was an Air Canada supervisor at DFW. We helped her with numerous tasks around her home in Plano, Texas. Lucy delighted in cooking and often invited us to try her untested recipes.

Utilizing our airline benefits, Frank and I flew to Canada, Thailand, Spain and the Virgin Islands. In Canada, we stayed in Quebec City, Montreal and Toronto. We flew on Thai Airlines to Bangkok. In Thailand, we took a bus trip to the infamous Burma Railway bridge on the Mae Klong River (also called Kwai Yai River), the basis for the movie *Bridge on the River Kwai.* By boat, we toured the floating market and cruised to the king's summer palace. We tried hot roasted locusts from the street vendors. It was a fascinating country with warmhearted people and good food.

Spain was our destination in the summer of 1980. We drove from Madrid to Santiago de Compostela on the northwestern coast, sleeping in elegant government-run *paradores* (former homes of counts and dukes). Santiago is the capital of Galicia and the *Catedral de Santiago* contains the remains of the apostle Saint James. Journeying by car gave us flexibility to stop at our leisure, ask for directions, go down a country road, inquire about a restaurant or ask a farmer what he was planting.

On our scheduled return flight on Iberia Airlines, we were "bumped" because all flights from Madrid to New York's JFK Airport were booked. With an extra day, we squeezed in an excursion to Toledo. The city sits on a mountain-top surrounded by the Tagus River. It is an architectural wonder: synagogues, mosques, cathedral, *alcázar* (fortress),

Roman bridges and city gates. Toledo is also the home of the famous Spanish painter *El Greco* ("The Greek") and where he created his best-known paintings.

When Karen moved to Everett, a Seattle suburb and home of Boeing, we had another incentive to fly to Seattle. She lived close to the Mukilteo ferry terminal from where we departed for Whidbey Island. Frank had a hard time pronouncing Mukilteo that led to teasing by all. With Cris, we drove to the Omak Stampede in eastern Washington State to watch those handsome cowboys.

Karen and I were good traveling companions. We vacationed in Australia, Europe, South America, U.S. cities and, of course, Minnesota. Continental Airlines was our carrier to Australia. We stayed in Double Bay, a chic section of Sydney. We hoped to visit the Great Barrier Reef, but the "hostesses" of the domestic airline were on strike. Sydney offered more to do than we had time for anyway, so it did not dampen our spirits. I quickly became comfortable driving on "the wrong side" of the road!

Additionally, we flew on BI to Ecuador to visit Carlos Harb in Quito who I met while traveling in Spain during my year abroad. He took us to Otavalo, home of the largest market in South America. We stopped at *La Linea* (the equator) and stood with one foot in each hemisphere! Carlos and I continued to explore Ecuador, after Karen's departure. We drove to Baños de Agua Santa, known as the "Gateway to the Amazon." Then all the way to coastal Guayaquil.

When Braniff opened a Los Angeles base for its new Pacific routes, Karen and I took advantage of that opportunity to fly to Guam, Hawaii, Singapore, Hong Kong and Seoul. We commuted from DFW to Los Angeles, often staying in Pasadena with Jim and Margaret Linscott. Frequently, we worked together as crew members on the same flights. Karen was an excellent lead flight attendant.

Layovers were often several days long, predominantly on overseas flights, so we had time to explore whatever that city had to offer.

On one layover in Hong Kong, a Chinese in-flight interpreter invited us to her home in Macau (a former Portuguese colony that is now part of China and a popular gambling mecca). We had an enchanting dinner and saw a significant part of the island. In Korea, we visited Panmunjom in the Joint Security Area at the DMZ (Demilitarized Zone) between North and South Korea. There was abundant shopping in Seoul. We purchased Korean chests, several pieces of rattan furniture, clocks, celadon, brass objects, tailor-made clothes and sneakers for family and friends.

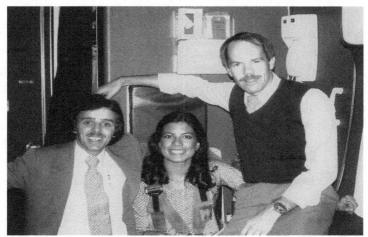

Flight Attendants – Jeff, Sheryl & David
747 flight from Los Angeles to Seoul, Korea, December 1979

Mother and Dad accompanied Karen and me on a trip to Hong Kong that included a layover of several days in Guam. Karen and I shared a crew room and gave the other to them. We drove along the scenic roads around the island, easily accomplished in a day, and relaxed in the sun on the beach or poolside.

Hong Kong offered unlimited possibilities, including shopping, delicious cuisine and spectacular scenery. We took a boat trip through the floating village at Aberdeen, walked through Tiger Balm Gardens and ate on a floating restaurant. We went by ferry from Kowloon to Hong Kong, followed by a cable tram ride up to Victoria Park. The view overlooking busy Hong Kong harbor was dramatic. Jewelry store owners that Karen and I befriended on previous layovers invited us to a local restaurant where we were the only Caucasians. Dad thoroughly delighted in the experience and even attempted to use chop sticks. They had clothing tailor-made and bought jewelry. During that trip we noticed the beginning signs of dementia in our father. He refused — was afraid — to be left alone, never letting us out of sight, and had difficulty making decisions.

Braniff friends were many and sadly several died of AIDS. We were in the middle of that horrible epidemic. There were some special BI comrades: Denise Miller, Jim Marcum, Merritt Crow, Steve Guarnaschelli, Pat Meadows, Bill Beckerich and Steve Pluta. Denise was a native Texan and with her distinct drawl, along with a smile, could tell a person "FU" without offending. Jim, Merritt, Pat and I were in the same class and often flew together. Steve Guarnaschelli was my roommate before I met Frank. Steve Pluta worked in the sales office. Bill, a flight attendant who had a pilot's license, took me along to fly in a single-engine plane around Dallas and on short flights within Texas. I learned a lot about flying and became skilled at "touch-and-goes." He and Karen helped move me from New York when I initially joined Braniff.

Much time was shared with Braniff co-workers. BI personnel had an incredible camaraderie that is typical of the industry. Karen and Evelynn Eubanks were kind to me and my colleagues, especially, when we first started flying. They helped us learn the tricks of the trade and often wined and dined us.

On May 12, 1982, Braniff International Airways ceased all operations — ending 54 years of air service — in order to meet financial obligations required by its ruthless rival, American Airlines. The "flying colors" era came to an abrupt halt when the airline declared bankruptcy. My crew was in Kansas City when the announcement was made. We arrived at DFW late in the evening aboard Braniff's last domestic flight. It was an eerie, heart-breaking, sight to see the colorful fleet parked at gates and on the tarmac at Terminal B. BI was the largest American company to cease operations.

David on stairs – Braniff 747 SP – Singapore – 1979

Chapter 11

DALLAS

Big "D" (little 'a,' double 'l,' 'a' 's') was good to me. In 1979, I purchased my first home at Birchbrook Condominium. Willie R Spencer, a former resident at The Castilian, recently bought a condominium at Birchbrook. She encouraged me to explore the possibility of moving there. Frank and I packed our belongings and moved from Cedar Springs across town. We shared this residence until sometime in 1981 when we agreed to separate. Our friendship, nevertheless, continued. He moved to the same apartment complex near DFW where Karen lived.

Willie R was a kind and generous neighbor. Her candor and wit made it delightful to be in her company. I remember her response to her son who inquired about her drinking alone: "I never drink alone. I have my first drink with Walter Cronkite and my second drink with Eyewitness News." Willie R was an excellent cook and liked to entertain. We were together many afternoons and evenings discussing a variety of topics. She, along with Lucy and me, had season tickets to the Dallas Opera. One summer, we drove from Texas to Minnesota to visit Mother and Dad. She enjoyed watching the children swim and water ski. On the fourth day, she insisted on leaving as planned, quoting Ben Franklin: "People are like fish. After three days they begin to smell." She returned to Minnesota in 1985 to attend my parents' 50th wedding anniversary.

Carol Morgan, an elementary school teacher, lived next door. She came from an established Dallas family. More than once, Frank and I took care of Peaches, her Old English Sheepdog. After she completed a summer program in North Carolina, I flew there to accompany her on the drive back to Texas. We stopped to tour the Biltmore Estate in Asheville,

North Carolina, the luxurious home of the Vanderbilts — a 250-room chateau with beautifully landscaped gardens.

Late one evening, Carol called me to go with her to her father's home. He had called her confused and crying (he suffered from dementia). When we arrived, coffee was all over the kitchen. He could not remember how to put the coffee maker together. About a year later, her father died while we were at the Morgan cottage in the mountains near Ruidoso, New Mexico. We went ahead with our dinner plans at the Inn of the Mountain Gods on the Mescalero Indian reservation. She flew home the next morning from El Paso. I drove her Toyota 280Z back to Dallas via country roads, with a stop at Carlsbad Caverns.

Ruth Guy lived below Carol. She regularly asked us to care for her dog, Dunkin. Dr. Guy was a retired pathologist and professor emeritus at the University of Texas Southwestern Medical School in Dallas. She was inducted into the Texas Women's Hall of Fame in 1989. Ruth recommended I keep a bottle of Gatorade in the refrigerator to calm an upset stomach. Ruth's favorite pastime was painting. One of her oils, a still life, hangs in my dining room. In 2003, a Christmas card from Ruth informed me that she could no longer see to read or write. Her letters were written by a caregiver.

Ann Foster was another Birchbrook neighbor whose condo was next door to Bill Anseley and Bill Winston. The three often entertained together. The Davis brothers lived directly above me. Jim was a cheerleader at Southern Methodist University and provided complimentary tickets to SMU football games. Following graduation, he became an American Airlines flight attendant.

Karen and I were treated by the same dermatologist, Coleman Jacobson. "Dr. J" adored Karen that led to invitations to Dallas Cowboy games as guests in his luxury suite at Texas Stadium. It was decadent sitting in a temperature-controlled room while being served complimentary cocktails and *hors d'oeuvres*.

There was one negative incident in Dallas: Bill Hunt and I were mugged. We were about to enter my car when two men approached us at gun point, demanding our wallets. Bill managed to enter the car, lock the doors and sound the car horn in one continuous blast. He was carrying a large sum of money from a fund-raising event. The man with the gun forced me to the ground and took my wallet. Then, the two ran to a waiting car, but not before we saw what they were wearing and a description of their car. I stopped a police cruiser that happened by within minutes of the incident and relayed what happened. Bill and I went into the house to calm our nerves. A police sergeant arrived within a half hour. He took us to identify the suspects that were picked up at a convenience store. One still had my easily recognized eel skin wallet. Bill asked the sergeant if the gun was loaded. He replied, "Affirmative." We pressed charges; however, the armed individual received a mere six-month sentence because local prisons were filled to capacity.

Dorothy Freedland, Dad's sister, developed a close relationship with Karen who frequently visited the Freedlands in Long Beach, California. In 1977, Dorothy, suffering from cancer, made her last trip to visit Karen and me. We had a pleasant time even though Dorothy struggled. At DFW, we assisted her to her seat on the Braniff aircraft. As soon as she was airborne, we walked to the nearest bar to toast her, knowing that we would not likely see her again. She died shortly after at age 56.

When Braniff International declared bankruptcy and ceased its operations in 1982, the college textbook division of Harcourt Brace Jovanovich Publishing Company (HBJ) became my employer. I attended training at HBJ's headquarters in San Diego, California. My assigned sales territory included colleges and universities within driving distance of the Dallas-Fort Worth area. That position required 100 per cent travel. Driving through small towns in the countryside was a joy. If not for HBJ, there were many places in the Lone Star state I would not have seen.

HBJ had an excellent array of textbooks. My responsibility was to convince professors and book committees to buy them. Many hours were devoted to meetings with professors who were cordial, for the most part. One professor at North Texas State University in Denton presented a challenge. He was arrogant and condescending. He later became a U.S. senator.

While working for HBJ, I took the required college courses for a Texas real estate license. I obtained certification and became affiliated with Jim Richardson Real Estate Agency. Timing could not have been worse. The real estate market suffered along with the Texas economy. Another agent with the firm was Parker Hall III. We became bosom buddies. The fact that he was fluent in Spanish made our bond stronger. Regrettably, I lost track of Parker who might have moved to Costa Rica where his mother resided.

Aside from Dallas, there were other Texas cities I found interesting. Fort Worth drew interest with its Kimbell Art Museum, water gardens, botanical gardens and stockades. It was a sophisticated metropolis, although some misrepresented it as a "cow town." San Antonio claimed the famous Alamo, in addition to seven or more other Spanish missions along the mission trail. Shops and countless Mexican restaurants lined the San Antonio River Walk. Austin lost some of its charm to growth, but the surrounding hill country was striking in springtime when blue bonnets and Indian paint brush were blooming. It was similar to Madison, Wisconsin: a state capital with a state university. Houston seemed more sociable than Dallas, even though it was larger.

The Texas landscape is as diverse as its inhabitants: pine forests in the east (known locally as "the piney woods"), tropical beaches on the Gulf of México, prairies in the north, hill country to the south and mountains in the west. Each area of that vast state is unique and known specifically for its products including cattle, cotton, fruit, commerce and, of course, "black gold."

Chapter 12

TRANS WORLD AIRLINES

There were many reasons that I left the publishing company to return to the airline industry, but the most significant was a desire to travel. Trans World Airlines hired me as a customer service agent (CSA) at Dallas-Fort Worth Airport in April 1984. My employment with TWA included several positions that ended at Philadelphia Airport in 1991.

At DFW, I met CSA Peter DiLemme. I cursed him when he transferred from Norfolk, as I had to handle many boxes he shipped before he moved to Texas. In spite of this, he more than made up for it during the time we worked and socialized together. Peter made me laugh when we worked together at the ticket counter where he persuaded me to participate in mischief that cannot be put in writing.

We planned to fly from JFK to Rome but, as standby passengers, were unable to obtain a flight to Italy. Without hesitation, we opted for a flight to England. We were in luck when a tour operator I knew from Travelers International, TWA's overseas tour company, met our flight at Heathrow Airport. She invited us to ride on the TI coach to London and stay as guests at the hotel where her group was booked. We participated in many tours with her group and made several side trips on our own.

After working one year at DFW, I was promoted to sales agent at the Dallas Sales Office (DSO). I served under the tutelage of Josanne Swain, a superb sales manager. Josanne never hesitated to share her knowledge to make my job easier. Our paths would cross many times over the years with TWA.

Josanne and I were given credit for arranging air travel to London for the first American Bowl, a contest between the Dallas Cowboys and Chicago Bears held at Wembley Stadium (August 03, 1986). Two TWA 747s were chartered: one each for the team and fans. I was assigned to escort the Cowboys with the purpose of verifying that all travel documents, including passports, were in order for both players and personnel. I flew to Thousand Oaks, California where the team trained, then accompanied them from Los Angeles to London several days in advance of the game. With four days of free time, I flew to Norway, stopping in Oslo and Bergen and, by ship, entered many fjords. At the last fjord, I disembarked to board a train to Oslo, passing through the picturesque Norwegian countryside past glaciers and waterfalls. I flew back to London to attend the game and sat on the 50-yard line! The Bears defeated the Cowboys 17 to 6.

Another benefit I received working in the DSO was to accompany VIP travel groups as a tour conductor. Twice, I led groups to Israel. The first consisted of born-again Christians, many of whom were hypocritical Baptist and Pentecostal ministers. Some drank alcohol discretely and, at times, they were disrespectful to their hosts. Their worst offense was at the Church of the Nativity in Bethlehem where they obnoxiously sang Christmas carols, ignoring the religious service in progress. In spite of some negative aspects, I made the most of it because it was my first visit to Israel.

Jeff Vance, my sister's stepson and a student of Saint Olaf College in Minnesota, was living and studying in Israel. Jeff invited me to join an expedition, led by an archeologist, to wadis (a dry stream bed except during periods of rainfall) near the Dead Sea, while the group I brought over toured another site. A swim in the Dead Sea was a highlight. The high mineral content — one of the world's saltiest bodies of water — made it impossible to sink. I read a newspaper while floating!

The second group I accompanied to Israel was definitely more fun. The majority were Catholic nuns representing different religious orders, mostly from Texas and Oklahoma. They were an orderly group that laughed, sang and were considerate of Israelis and Palestinians.

I met Bud Noble — my lifetime partner — while affiliated with the DSO. Two mutual friends, Bill Hunt and Parker Hall, introduced us at the Arena, a gay dance bar in Dallas. For Bud, I used another TWA privilege: emergency authority to adjust air fares. When Mary Noble, Bud's mother, was gravely ill, I reserved his roundtrip flights to Indianapolis only days before his departure at the lowest published fare. (Chapter 13 provides a detailed description of Bud.)

My third year with TWA, I was promoted to supervisor at the Getaway Tour Center in Philadelphia. In April 1987 the company moved Bud and me, lock, stock and barrel — even liquor and an eight-foot-long flower box filled with dirt! Bud was not working full time, consequently, when the opportunity to move to Philadelphia occurred, he eagerly went along. The eleven-year Dallas chapter came to a close.

The Getaway Center opened a door to see various destinations: a Mediterranean cruise that combined several Greek islands and coastal Turkey, twice to Israel and London several times. Most trips were VIP tours for large travel agencies that did business with TWA and required an accompanying TWA representative. Each year, there were also familiarization trips for the reservation staff that was led by a supervisor.

I combined travel privileges with Bill Bischoff, a Getaway supervisor. Our first departure took us to Amsterdam, but our favorite was to Germany in December. We began in Munich to experience *Krisskringlemarkt* where one could enjoy food, shop and the ambience of an open-air holiday Christmas market. That was followed by a visit to Berlin not long before the wall came down. East German police boats suspiciously patrolled the Spree River separating East and West Berlin. We took a train into East Berlin where the East German police hassled Bill for some unknown reason. Once on the other side, we had a positive experience with no more challenges. We easily recognized the austerity of East Germany.

The most memorable benefit I received, compliments of TWA, comprised a seven-day cruise from Philadelphia to Bermuda aboard the *Ocean Princess* in September 1987. Bud unselfishly gave up his opportunity to go with me so that I could take Mother. For her, the timing was significant as Dad had recently moved to an Alzheimer's facility. Karen flew with Mother from Minneapolis to Philadelphia. Bud and Karen briefly came aboard to see our accommodations before we began our cruise down the Delaware River from Penn's Landing.

Vivian & David
Aboard the *Ocean Princess* – September 1987

We sailed down the C & D (Chesapeake and Delaware) Canal, anchoring in Annapolis. Cousin Marilyn met us at the pier. The intermediate stop provided sufficient time to tour the Naval Academy and eat lunch at a French restaurant before our ship raised anchor.

Jay Walsh, a Getaway tour agent, and his friend Richard Black, shared a table with us at the second seating for dinner, each night. They were very attentive to Mother on the entire cruise. Most evenings, we joined them in their cabin to drink champagne that Jay brought on board.

Bermuda had recently been struck by a hurricane. Due to the aftermath of the storm, there were several hours of rough seas that resulted in seasick passengers, but none in our group became ill. Trees and utility lines were still down when we arrived. Fortunately, we were able to shop and tour the island. Mother even rode on a moped! The voyage provided an opportunity for Mother to relax and revitalize.

Karen and I planned to meet friends for *Oktoberfest* in 1988. Bud drove us to JFK. He discovered that all TWA flights to Germany were oversold, while we were getting travel documents. As non-revenue passengers, we had no chance of boarding a flight to Germany, so we changed our documents and flew to Switzerland!

For two enlightening weeks, we traveled around the country on efficient Swiss trains. Our first stop was Lucerne. We liked that city so much that we extended our stay. When we arrived in Zermatt, the weather was dismal. We were told that the sun had not shone in more than two weeks. To our delight, we woke to crystal-clear skies with the magnificent Matterhorn plainly visible. We took a cog train to a chalet at the base of the Matterhorn and had lunch in full view of the mountain. In the capital of Bern, our last stop in the country, we bought cuckoo clocks and music boxes. We were impressed with the overall beauty, cleanliness and incomparable Swiss efficiency.

While in Switzerland, I realized the extent to which Karen's vision had deteriorated. When I excitedly pointed out vistas from the train window, she candidly told me that she could not see them. If we were not moving, she had time to focus, so objects could usually be seen. She never complained about her condition nor did it detract from our travels. From that point on, however, I used discretion.

Bud and I vacationed in Egypt in March 1989, compliments of TWA and Travelers International. At Cairo Airport, our TI guide met us holding a sign for "Mr. and Mrs. Peterson." Once that was explained away, he drove us to our hotel. The next day, we embarked on a multi-day Nile cruise aboard the five-star *Seti III*. Numerous stops were made to walk about the ancient sites of Abu Simbel, Luxor, Aswan and Cairo, places that swept us off our feet. In Cairo, our driver took us to the pyramids at Gisa and photographed me riding a camel led by Bud Noble! The Egyptians were gracious and their antiquities were indescribable.

David on camel led by Bud!
Gisa, Egypt – 1989

We met Margaret and Roy Mole, an English couple from London, on the Nile cruise. An immediate bond was established. A catalyst to our connection may have had something to do with the fact that we were in a minority on that vessel: we versus the French. In the years that followed, whenever I conducted a tour group to London, I attempted to find time to join them.

A year later, my birthday gift to Bud was a trip to England. Without his knowledge, Roy and Margaret arranged for us to stay in their home in Surrey. Bud was pleasantly surprised when told to bring his bags from their car into the house. We experienced many things from a truly English perspective, including "authentic" breakfasts, and dinners that were followed with Stilton cheese and balanced with Port. How civilized! Although we may speak the same language, we discovered that there were many cultural differences.

We strolled along the Thames to Hampton Court, a lengthy walk from the Moles. A British Rail representative and TWA associate provided us with free rail passes. That enabled us to go by rail on several trips in and out of London and to Oxford to retrace steps I made there in the seventies with my Kiwi companions.

TWA filed for bankruptcy in January 2001 and was acquired by American Airlines. TWA, in a sense, was reborn in May 2019, with the opening of a 500 room first class hotel at JFK Airport. MCR and MORSE developed the hotel in the historic 1962 Eero Saarinen's TWA airline terminal. *Connie,* the Lockheed Constellation aircraft and pride of TWA's fleet, built in the 1940s, was transported and placed inside the hotel as a restaurant. That plane served as Air Force One for President Dwight Eisenhower in the 1950s.

Chapter 13

BUD NOBLE

Mason "Bud" Noble V is my partner and spouse. He was born on September 23, 1948 in Rochester, New York, the son of Mason Noble IV and Mary Prentiss Loder. Bud is the youngest of four children. His siblings are Cathryn, Mary (Penny) and Ann. When Bud was a young child, the Nobles moved from New York to Fort Wayne, Indiana where he spent most of his youth. The family moved to Ohio, for a seven-year period, then returned to the Fort Wayne area. Bud graduated in 1966 from Sylvania High School outside Toledo, Ohio.

Bud received a Bachelor of Music in 1971 from Muskingum College in New Concord, Ohio, a private liberal arts college affiliated with the Presbyterian Church. He later returned to Fort Wayne to continue his education at Indiana University–Purdue University Fort Wayne (IPFW) and received a BA in accounting from Indiana University in 1981. Bud was accomplished on the French horn and was a member of the Fort Wayne Philharmonic.

Our relationship began in August 1986 in Dallas, Texas. We were legally married on December 16, 2014 in Exton, Chester County, Pennsylvania.

Meeting Bud is the most wonderful thing that ever happened to me. He is a man of principles, honest to a fault and generous in every sense of the word. He goes out of his way to help people and supports many causes that he deems appropriate. Recipients of his generosity include former colleges, the USO and numerous other organizations. It is difficult for him to say "no" when a solicitor calls asking for a donation. Bud is very idealistic and would like to solve the world's problems. He epitomizes the saying: "… would give you the shirt off his back." He may be impatient at times, but offsets it with compassion. Another characteristic is his sensitivity. Bud is easily gladdened, annoyed, or pained by external influences that often move him to tears. Still, he has a humorous side that easily moves him, and others, to laughter.

Bud is loquacious. Initially, he may be quiet because he is genuinely timid. Once he knows a person, it might be difficult to get a word in edgewise. He does not intentionally control a conversation, although it may happen when he attempts to get across his point or he is passionate about the subject at hand. To his credit, he is well read and knowledgeable on many subjects and can support his points of view. He has an excellent memory and an innate ability to conceptualize.

As a team, we have literally been through thick and thin. Each has had his turn in helping the other, whether for emotional or physical support. Bud nurtured me following thyroid surgery and throughout a difficult bout with Lyme disease. He supported me during stressful employment I endured under a micro manager at an anesthesiology group. He helped me face the death of my father, mother and brother. Appreciation and gratitude go to Bud for his support while I was away helping Jim during his final days.

During our relationship Bud has lost both of his parents. His mother died of cancer the first year we were together. His father died of a stroke in December 1997. Together, we endured his recovery and physical therapy following his total knee replacement. We did the same when he was struck by a hit-and-run taxi while riding his bicycle and suffered a broken collar bone. Bud withstood more than his share of stress from job layoffs, a common phenomenon of non-profit agencies.

Meeting Bud's friends gave me an extended family. He shared an apartment with Steve Hall when we first met. They were confidants and Steve soon became mine. Steve had an extremely quick wit. He was an excellent country western dancer. The Round Up Saloon was our dance floor of choice for Texas two-stepping. A memorable time with Steve was attending the AIDS fund raiser "AIDS Is a Drag." Our "drag" consisted of western attire. He remarked to Bud about his surprise at the number of people I knew. The two prepared an elaborate Thanksgiving feast. Seventeen men were at the dinner table. The Texas Gay Rodeo presented another chance to be together. Those "cowboys" were serious competitors.

Steve and I might have become an item if Bud had not cemented our relationship. Steve remarked that he was waiting for us to go our separate ways (Bud had a reputation for short term affairs). Admittedly, we did have a mutual admiration.

In any event, Steve met Bill Haller and they developed a permanent relationship. Employment opportunities led to their move to Las Vegas. On a trip to Nevada, they drove us to Zion National Park, stopping to take an extensive tour of Hoover Dam. Zion presented many breath-taking views. To me, it rivaled the beauty of the Grand Canyon. We traversed three states — Nevada, Arizona and Utah — within a few hours where the states conjoin. Bill and Steve retired in the foothills of the Rincon Mountains outside Tucson.

We visited their home — a unique adobe structure — on Pistol Hill Road. Coyotes, foxes, mountain goats, mule deer, quail and snakes could be seen near their house. Bill built a half-mile long path from the house into the adjacent *arroyos* that wound around saguaro cactuses and into ravines. It was "paved" with pebbles he hauled in by wheelbarrow and lined with large stones. Benches were placed strategically where one could stop to meditate. Each resting place was set aside for a specific person, including one each for his two daughters. I spent quality time on the path. A daily ritual was to walk its length at least once. We lost Steve to AIDS in 2000. He was fortunate to survive that disease for many years.

Other friends I met through Bud included Don Dent, Dwight Matthews, Mark Covington and Dennis LeClech. Don, Dwight and Dennis died of AIDS. Don, with his partner Marion Weger, owned Gratitude, a vintage clothing shop in Dallas' trendy Oak Lawn. Don liked cold weather and scheduled winter trips to visit us in Philly, then continued to New York City and Boston. Dwight was a very attractive man. Many years, he won a high heel race at a Halloween festival that drew crowds from every walk of life. Mark moved to New Mexico and finally settled in Palm Springs, California. Dennis worked as a sales agent for China Air Lines. He moved back to Seattle to spend his final days with his family. I visited him shortly before his death. We toast Dennis whenever we drink from a China Air Lines mug.

When we moved to Philadelphia in 1987, Bud made a commitment to visit his father and stepmother, Mase and Dottie, in Connecticut. Following Mase's death, we continued that promise and helped Dottie with tasks in her home. We worked countless hours assisting her when she sold her Simsbury home (of forty years). That required driving to Connecticut most every weekend for two months.

The evening of Mason Noble IV's funeral, Dottie took Cathy, Penny, Ann, Bud and me to dinner at a lovely restaurant in Avon, Connecticut. It was an opportunity to be alone, along with some very special exchanges. The Nobles gave Dottie a beautiful amethyst brooch, an heirloom from their mother. Dottie gave me Mase's black onyx ring that was symbolic of my relationship to Dottie and the Nobles, plus a reminder of an identical ring my father used to wear. Dad's ring disappeared in a nursing home, otherwise it would have been given to me. By chance, we all wore the same size ring.

Bud's employment history has been diverse and numerous. He taught instrumental music at Prairie Heights High School in Angola, Indiana, after graduating from Muskingum College. Subsequent positions were mostly with non-profit organizations utilizing his accounting degree. In Philadelphia, he served as an accountant with The Berman Group, controller of the architectural firm of Feltoon Perry Associates, administrative director of the AIDS Information Network, volunteer coordinator of the AIDS Walk and operations director for Community Women's Education Project. He "cleaned up" accounting problems that he inherited, then tackled the next challenge. For two years, he commuted by train to Lancaster where he was the business office manager of the Lancaster Surgery Center.

In 1998, Bud was hired as a healthcare systems consultant at Shared Medical Systems (SMS). In his last position he served as a financial analyst. In the fall of 2002, Bud was a victim of downsizing. He soon obtained another position as a financial analyst, his expertise always landed him a new position.

Bud's greatest passions are music and reading, followed closely by cycling. When Bud is not reading, he is most likely listening to music. A shared interest in music explains our annual subscription to the Philadelphia Orchestra. At one time, his extensive library included a large selection of gay literature. The latter portion was donated to the Barbara Gitting's Archives of the Philadelphia Free Library.

Cycling is an obsession for Bud. When we moved to the suburbs, he rode more frequently and with a greater choice of destinations. He joined at least two bicycle clubs and subscribed to several cycling magazines. He continues to ride the streets and trails of the Philly area today — weather permitting, three to four times a week, throughout the year — on his multicolored Colnago road bike.

David Peterson

Bud on Colnago road bike – August 2005

I would be remiss not to mention that our mutual interest in music greatly influenced our first trip and, most likely, contributed to our lasting relationship. In short, we were discussing music and my participation in the Minnesota Marching Band. The conversation led to the Indiana State School Music Association (ISSMA), the organization that coordinates the annual state marching band competition at the Hoosier Dome in Indianapolis. Bud asked if I would be interested in going with him to the ISSMA competition in November. Without hesitation, I answered with a resounding "yes." That was 1986, and I continued going almost every year. Bud has attended those events since 1973 and, amazingly, missed only one competition.

I met people that Bud sat with every year at those competitions. John Price, another avid marching band fan, lived in Indianapolis and invited us to spend the weekends of the event at his home. I always looked forward to the lunch breaks that included a beer or two with Josh

Bartrom, Wes Barnes, Joe Roy and Jason Jaworski. All four were schoolmates from Fort Wayne that created a common bond with Bud. I found it heartening to feel completely comfortable with them, and the feelings appeared to be mutual.

Josh, Joe, Wes & Jason
ISSMA – Hoosier Dome – November 2013

Chapter 14

PHILADELPHIA

Philadelphia is the metropolitan area in which I have lived the longest. In 1987, Bud and I moved from Dallas to Center City where we resided for thirteen years. Employment opportunities resulted in a move to the suburbs in 2000. We moved back to Philadelphia in 2015 following Bud's retirement.

Our first residence in Center City was on 9th Street, a block from Pennsylvania Hospital, in a quiet residential neighborhood close to the Historic District (Independence Hall, Carpenters Hall and the Liberty Bell), Society Hill, Washington Square and Penn's Landing. Pennsylvania Hospital, the nation's oldest and perhaps most beautiful hospital, was one block away. Despite three flights of stairs, the location made it appealing and convenient for our guests. Our unit comprised the top two floors of an early 19th century house that was converted into six apartments. It had hardwood floors, nooks and crannies to place artifacts, beautiful staircases and a good view from our windows. We had a New Year's Eve party our first year with over ninety people attending.

Joe Fontana and Jeff Davis renovated a house two blocks away on Camac Street that became a showcase. They used our place to shower during the renovation. Bud and I dined with them on a regular basis until they moved to Florida. Cris and Neal met Joe when they were visiting from Seattle. She referred to him as an Italian stallion (he was very attractive and physically striking).

Joe introduced us to Kay LaHusen and Barbara Gittings. They lived on the infamous Osage Street (home of the MOVE organization). The Mummers parade was a New Year's Day tradition, standing in the cold on the steps of the Academy of Music, watching the string bands march by. Those two brave women were gay pioneers involved in the founding of LGBT organizations. Barbara was a prominent activist for LGBT equality and participated in the first picket lines for that cause in front of Independence Hall in the 1960s.

The Arches, a town house community at 22nd Street, became our second residence. It was convenient to West River Drive that winds along the Schuylkill River. On weekends, that picturesque tree-lined drive was closed for recreation, so we joined throngs of people riding our bikes around the eight-mile circuit.

Pat Ciarrocchi, a local television news anchor, lived above us. Although a petite lady, slightly more than five feet tall when stretching, we knew when she was home as she walked overhead in her high heels. Pat had a refreshing disposition and always wore a smile. She announced her engagement, one evening, with a knock on our door and holding three goblets and a bottle of wine. We were thrilled when she invited us to her wedding in the Rose Room at the Belleview Hotel — the infamous Legionnaires Disease hotel. A monsignor and rabbi ministered the wedding ceremony. An elaborate reception followed with dinner and dancing. For collecting her mail, while she was in Italy on her honeymoon with David Fineman, she gave us an Italian brass corkscrew that we use to this day!

Jeff Jones lived across the courtyard with his Springer Spaniel, Samantha. When necessary, we were more than happy to walk his four-legged friend. We frequently accompanied Jeff to his favorite restaurant in his native New Jersey. The Pub opened in 1951. Although a typical east coast diner, it was known for its unusually good food, in spite of its massive size. Its dining room could accommodate five hundred people.

Pat Pitt was a neighbor when we lived at The Arches. Bud referred to her as the "P" lady due the following alliteration: Pat Pitt served in the Peace Corps in Panamá and lived on Panama Street in Philadelphia, Pennsylvania. We are happy to have her as our neighbor, once again, two blocks from our current home in Center City.

Many occasions, often spur of the moment, are enjoyed with Terry Wetsel. When we lived at The Arches, his apartment was across town in the Hopkinson House on Washington Square. A favorite view was from his 26th floor balcony that faced south towards the airport with the Delaware River in view.

Lou Partridge was one of the first people we met in Philadelphia. He knew my UW colleague Tony Cardenas who was once married to one of Lou's co-workers. We had dinner at his home when Tony came to town on a business trip. Lou enjoys organizing dinner dates and excursions. We joined him on a day trip to New York City to visit the Hispanic Society and the Cloisters Museum.

In 1998, Bud celebrated his 50th birthday in a generous way at the Napoleon Restaurant on Broad Street. He invited friends to join him for cocktails and dinner. Don Dent came all the way from Dallas to honor him. That was Bud's biggest celebration.

My sister Karen lived in Center City in 2001 at Penn Center House, a cooperative apartment at 1900 JFK Boulevard. Coincidentally, it is visible from our balcony today. We made many improvements to her apartment. Dinner included Karen on nights we went to a Philadelphia Orchestra concert. Karen moved to Minneapolis to be closer to Mother.

Chapter 15

EMPLOYMENT IN PENNSYLVANIA

My employment in Philadelphia began as a supervisor with TWA at the Getaway Tour Center in April 1987. The reservation sales office occupied an entire floor in the Rohm & Haas Building across from Independence Hall. I walked past that historic building and the Liberty Bell every day on my way to work. I transferred to Philadelphia Airport (PHL) and supervised customer service agents and, of course, resolved customer complaints. A favorite responsibility involved meeting an on-time departure of our daily flight to London. Working at PHL was my most satisfying airline position. I liked dealing with the challenges it offered but appreciated the rewards.

With TWA's impending bankruptcy, I made a career change to the medical field in 1991. An anesthesiology group hired and trained me as an account representative at a free-standing ambulatory surgery center in New Jersey. Medical coding was the most interesting part of that job. A Tennessee company purchased the surgery center about a year later. The new owners promoted me as their business office manager responsible for all non-medical functions and personnel. The same anesthesiology group rehired me a year later and placed me at Wills Eye Hospital in Center City where I performed third-party billing. I worked closely with OR staff and wore comfortable green hospital scrubs.

During employment at Wills Eye, I was diagnosed with hypothyroidism and Hashimoto's disease (an autoimmune disorder in which the immune system attacks the thyroid). Further testing detected hyperparathyroidism and an adenoma in my thyroid that required surgery. Endocrinologist Anne de Papp referred me to a renowned surgeon at

Thomas Jefferson University Hospital. Dr. Herb Cohen successfully performed both a parathyroidectomy and a partial thyroidectomy. Terry helped Bud with my discharge from the hospital. I soon discovered the pain of sneezing following throat surgery. I thought the sutures were ripped open when that first happened! The offending get well bouquet of fragrant lilacs was quickly removed. Recovery was speedy and, in a matter of weeks, my fatigue subsided.

Thanks to encouragement from a Jefferson surgeon, I left Wills Eye Hospital in 1997 and accepted a position in the Otolaryngology Department (ENT: ear, nose and throat) at Thomas Jefferson University Hospital. I supervised patient registration and gained excellent experience that served as a steppingstone to my final working career. After only one year, I seized an opportunity to increase my salary and accept a more challenging position.

In 1998, within a few months of each other, Bud and I accepted positions at Shared Medical Systems. Bud joined a group as a healthcare systems consultant (HSC) that supported Allegra products, a specific hospital software. I joined the Berwyn field office as a patient accounting HSC. Phil Fretz was a key player in obtaining that position. He had worked with SMS several years and submitted my resume to the branch office where I was hired. I reported to Stephen DeFruscio, a knowledgeable and organized manager, undoubtedly the best of my entire career. The role required 90 percent travel and the complexity of the product made it very challenging. The rewards were the people I met, both co-workers and employees at the sites. Diana Bierds, a senior patient accounting consultant, was my mentor.

For more than a year, I commuted daily to Lancaster General Hospital. Early one morning, Karen Brooks, the hospital's patient accounting manager with whom I was working as a consultant, met me at the office door. She told me that SMS had called instructing me to contact my mother. I was informed that Dad had died that morning (January 19, 1999). Karen invited me into her office where I broke down into uncontrollable sobbing. Once I regained my composure, I drove home to arrange a flight to Minnesota.

Pat Whitehead met my flight in Minneapolis. That cold January day she drove my sister Karen and me to Sauk Centre. We witnessed cars slide off Interstate 94 into the snow. A private memorial service was held at the Methodist Church. A luncheon following the service was open to the public. Because Dad had suffered many years from dementia, I did not anticipate that his death would be as difficult to accept. Still, there was relief knowing that his agony, and Mother's, had come to an end.

My second SMS position was with the Provider Billing department. I worked from home as a provider billing consultant (PBC) supporting SMS' hospital customers in twelve southern states and Puerto Rico. All correspondence was done by phone or via Internet using a laptop computer. Knowledge of Spanish was a considerable asset in dealing with Puerto Rican customers. Although my knowledge of patient accounting continued to grow with experience, customer service skills led to my success. One Texas hospital contacted my supervisor to express appreciation for my assistance. That resulted in an award and set of crystal champagne glasses. I was fluted!

It was good fortune to be working at home because I contracted Lyme Disease in June 2000, while working at the Noble cottage. After the initial few weeks of sick leave, I worked half days with many naps in between. Kathy Stripay, my manager, and co-workers were very supportive. The long recovery lingered into November. I remember little of that summer. "Bud Nightingale" helped me throughout that ordeal. Because I slept most of the time, he took advantage of his freedom — with my encouragement — to cycle Pennsylvania roadways.

One enjoyable PBC project was commuting to Michigan to install software at the Detroit Medical Center. The best part of that assignment was working with SMS team members Barb, Elaine and Scott. After the Detroit project, I supported various SMS hospitals while waiting to transition to another division within the company. SMS made it easy to move to other areas if it were a benefit to both parties concerned. I held three different positions in a relatively short time with the company.

The last job title I held with SMS was systems analyst, specifically, methodology developer, for patient accounting software implementation. I performed well in that role because it provided a chance to demonstrate creative writing skills and work with detail. Most responsibilities involved writing and editing documentation of company products. My office was in the corporate headquarters complex close to my colleague Phil.

Many SMS employees lived "high on the hog," especially those in field offices. Unlimited expense accounts and extravagant award dinners and conferences were common. When I initially worked in a field office, I attended a group event on Cape Cod that included two days at an exclusive resort, a lobster dinner and paid air transportation. Siemens, the German conglomerate and one of the largest companies in the world, purchased SMS in 2001. In order to run the company from a business point of view, many changes were put in place, but it was a slow process changing the mindset of old timers.

I retired from Siemens in May 2002. I was indeed delighted when Joe Steiniger, my financial consultant, advised me that I could turn in my badge. Because I had been practical with money, early retirement became a reality. I earned it! It was a good decision made with no regrets.

Mental relaxation was first on my agenda. However, physical rest did not happen for some time, as Bud and I worked hard at the Noble cottage that spring and early summer. I enjoyed that work: outdoors swinging an ax, digging with a shovel, using a rake, pushing a lawn mower, painting and making repairs to the cottage.

In retirement, I planned part-time work to supplement my income and occupy spare time. I taught English as a second language to adults in the Hispanic community of Kennett Square, twenty-five miles from our home. The evening classes required considerable preparation to do a good job. An affinity for that culture and the students' eagerness to learn made it rewarding. Lamentably, the long commute convinced me to leave that position when the course concluded.

Bud suggested I apply at the nearby Home Depot in Frazer. Soon, I was working as a part-time associate in the seasonal department that gave me an opportunity to work with interesting personnel and serve the public. Curiously, on more than one occasion, customers — male and female — attempted to seduce me, but that was not the "service" I was hired to perform! I did not mind the physical activity (lifting and carrying objects and standing on my feet all day), but it was the pollutants throughout the warehouse that eventually forced me to resign, as I developed asthmatic symptoms. I left on good terms and put Home Depot's slogan to rest: "You can do it. [I] can help."

No grass grew under my feet. I was soon "minding the farm" for my cousin in Chester, Maryland on the Eastern Shore of the Chesapeake Bay. The Wilsons had three horses, a dog, two cats, a koi pond and a large lawn. The horses required considerable attention: feeding twice a day, putting out to pasture and mucking their stalls. I became very skilled at driving Hal's tractor, pulling the manure spreader and mowing. Caring for the Wilson's property became a regular routine whenever they were away. On many occasions, I did the same for Phil, a frequent traveler, at his house in Delaware, caring for his dogs and garden.

Widgets, a small privately owned company, needed office help. It was conveniently located two miles from our home. The company produced specialty items — t-shirts, caps, pens, et cetera with the organization's name or logo printed on them — mostly for local fire and police departments. In the fall of 2004, I began a three-year assignment handling billing and data entry duties.

When Widgets no longer needed my help, I landed a job as a driver for Heritage Coach Company, a dealer of hearses and limousines. I drove new vehicles to funeral homes located mainly in Delaware, Maryland, New Jersey and Pennsylvania. However, there were trips to

Boston, Indiana and one as far as Iowa. After each delivery, I either drove a trade-in or flew back to the corporate office. One New Jersey funeral business ordered two gold hearses to match its existing fleet of the same color. It was an agreeable position that offered an opportunity to see more of the country.

Chapter 16

LIFE IN CHESTER COUNTY

In January 2000, Bud and I relocated to suburban Malvern in Chester County, Pennsylvania, our home for almost fifteen years. We were reluctant to leave Center City, but the twenty-five-mile commute to SMS was too arduous. Malvern borough was a quaint little place with antique shops, a drug store, a cobbler and a small strip mall. We knew it could not replace Center City living, but its location was a priority. The biggest drawback of the suburbs was that a vehicle was required to go anywhere outside our development. There were no sidewalks!

Through diligent searching, Bud found a townhouse to our liking in Northridge, a community of forty-four homes. The development was located on a ridge overlooking Great Valley, two miles to SMS and one-half mile to the regional rail station. We had one month to paint, install hardwood floors and kitchen cabinets, replace the second-floor carpeting and purchase appliances. The townhouse was larger than our Center City apartment but had a similar floor plan that made it easy to arrange and accommodate our furniture.

We soon became acquainted with residents of the community. That was by and large made easier after we began to walk the circular road with our dog. In August 2002 our lives changed overnight when we adopted a little German boy named Chuck! That perfectly marked black and tan, miniature, smooth Dachshund was a joy and a challenge. It was a constant battle to overcome his separation anxiety. Chuck had a beautiful gait and held his high — a showstopper. He did not know a stranger, canine or human. Chuck was affectionately referred to as "Mayor of

101

Northridge." He bonded with all dogs. In spite of his size, he was the alpha. Karen's K-9 became his favorite place away from home for day care and boarding. We were totally smitten by that little guy with his unconditional love. Sadly, our days with Chuck were not meant to last as he had an incurable disc disease; consequently, he was euthanized.

David and Chuck – August 2002

Amanda Bezon and Tim Shine were two residents with whom we shared much time. Her dog Murphy, a large 90-pound black Doberman-Labrador mix, and Chuck were best friends, a comical duo when playing or walking together. Their relationship carried over to the three adults. Tim cycled with Bud. He delighted having folks over, especially during football season. Amanda and Tim were witnesses in our wedding.

We were members of The Chester County Brunch Bunch, an organization mostly made up of the LGBT community that met monthly. It celebrated its 20th anniversary in January 2009. The Brunch introduced us to many people.

We met Phil Fretz at one of the first brunches we attended and a lasting friendship developed. Phil worked with me at SMS. He and his partner owned a home in Ocean View, Delaware near the Indian River Bay, a huge expanse of water popular for recreation. After many improvements, they sold it and relocated to Lewes, a few miles north of Rehoboth Beach. We witnessed his two daughters grow up, and we attended their weddings.

Karen and I cared for Phil's two dogs at the Ocean View home in the summer of 2002. The weather was extremely hot with violent thunderstorms, one producing a record six inches of rain. We sat in a protected screened porch during the storm with dogs at our sides. Many roads were temporarily closed due to flooding. In October of that year, my sister Sue and I visited Phil. She waded, for the first time, in the Atlantic Ocean and did it two days in a row: once at the Delaware Seashore State Park and again at Bethany Beach.

Bob and Lee lived in Devon, a mere five miles from our home. We shared considerable time with them as dinner guests or caring for Bob in Lee's absence. (Bob suffered a stroke requiring 24-hour care.) I resided at their house, for one month, when Lee was recovering from chicken pox. There were now two requiring attention and a house to maintain! More than once, our schedules allowed us to accept an invitation to relax at their winter home in Key West.

One couple had elaborate brunches, particularly on New Year's Eve. Their house had an indoor and outdoor swimming pool and a beautifully landscaped yard. Together, we attended a concert featuring Barbara Cook — an American actress and singer who gained fame for her Broadway leads in *Candide*, 1956 and *The Music Man*, 1957 — at the

David Peterson

Merriam Theatre, and saw *Into the Woods*, starring Bernadette Peters and Tommy Tune, at the Forrest Theatre.

Meals were a joint preparation with two friends in West Chester, Pennsylvania. Some were exotic, including one that required cleaning and cooking squid. There were many trips to Bethany Beach, Delaware to stay at their condo, one block from the Atlantic. I used the ocean as a therapeutic way to cleanse my soul, spending hours swimming or walking along the beach. They introduced us to acquaintances that were new power boat owners. We accompanied them aboard their 44-foot yacht on the Chesapeake Bay that provided an opportunity to explore and dine at bayside communities.

We spent time with a couple in Coatesville. One afternoon, I arrived at their home, while they were at work, unlocked the door and punched in the code to disarm the security system. Within minutes, the alarm sounded. It took me awhile to switch it off. The alarm company called requesting a password, which I had forgotten. Soon, two — not one — black and white Coatesville police cruisers arrived. It appeared obvious to the police that I entered legitimately: dogs were at my side; I took bags *into* the house; I wore a coat and tie; I possessed a key; and I provided an adequate explanation. I committed that password to memory!

When one was dying of AIDS, I cared for him on a day his partner needed to work. Holding nothing more than skin and bones, I carried him to the bathroom. He was clinging to a last bit of dignity.

Our most eccentric but likeable Brunch group acquaintance graduated with Longwood Gardens' first horticulture class. We met John when he was director of the Conestoga House in Lancaster. Bud worked nearby at the Lancaster Surgery Center. John opened up his home for Bud to recuperate after arthroscopic knee surgery. When the Conestoga House no longer challenged him, he decided to plant new roots and open a store in San Diego. It required two tractor trailers to move his treasures! I helped him pack his collection of antiquities and garden paraphernalia.

A Mind of his Own

Twice, Bud and I visited him in California. Eventually, he moved back to Chester County.

Vadim Cantón, a psychiatrist and son of my friend Alex, attended a medical seminar in Philadelphia. He stayed with us at the conclusion of his meetings. He managed to visit the Philadelphia Museum of Art, the historic area and Valley Forge National Park. One evening, we looked at transparencies of the time I spent in Panamá. Because of Vadim's interest in the photos, I gave the appropriate ones to him. I also offered him a $20.00 sterling silver balboa (Panamanian currency) commemorative coin that I purchased in the 1970s. He and his wife Valeria visited us the following year.

Cris LeGassey made a long overdue trip east in September 2006. She took Bud and me to see the musical ensemble Pink Martini at the Keswick Theatre. That was our first introduction to the group which she had followed for years. She requested that one day be dedicated to Lancaster County's Amish country that was a highlight of her visit. The night before her departure, we invited many to bid her farewell.

Molly Stainton was an acquaintance for at least seven years when we had a momentous revelation, sometime in 2010. I noticed a framed photograph, in her living room, of the Fairbanks House in Dedham, Massachusetts. That home was built by ancestors of mine in 1636. I inquired why she had that photograph. She replied: "I *am* a Fairbanks." We discovered that we were distant cousins! Molly was trained as a nurse and served in Hawaii during WWII.

Roy and Margaret Mole thrilled us with a visit to Malvern in May 2011 to celebrate their 60th wedding anniversary! It was their first visit to "The Colonies." They stayed for two fun-filled weeks. Their arrival was timed perfectly to attend a Philadelphia Orchestra performance featuring The *Planets* by the English composer Gustav Holst. They toured the Philadelphia area extensively. In Delaware, they enjoyed the historic town of Lewes named after a village in the United Kingdom. A highlight for Margaret was "paddling" in the Atlantic Ocean at Rehoboth Beach.

Roy was fascinated by War of Independence monuments. He found it curious that we — Americans — generally refer to that conflict as the Revolutionary War. Both are avid readers. Every day, Roy enjoyed reading the *Philadelphia Inquirer*, usually outside on the deck.

Bud and David – 20 years – August 9, 2006

Chapter 17

JOURNEYS

Philadelphia, strategically located on the northeast coast, made travel relatively easy to New York, New England, Annapolis and Washington, D.C. It was a two-hour ride to visit John Marken in Queens. Bud stayed with John during the 1994 Gay Games that were held in New York City. I joined him for the closing ceremonies at Yankee Stadium. Barbara Cook sang at the ceremonies.

It was always special to visit "cuz" Marilyn. Our relationship began in the 1970s when I lived in Forest Hills, New York. Marilyn and Hal lived in Athol, Massachusetts with their young children, Lee and Grant. I drove to Athol several times to see them. When a new career opportunity arose for Hal in Washington, D.C., the Wilsons moved to Annapolis in 1977 where they resided in Admiral Heights for more than twenty years.

Bud and I enjoyed our visits to Annapolis, especially when sailing in their fast 33-foot sailboat Leewind. In one race with Marilyn, Bud and me as crew, we were in first place until Hal tacked short of the last buoy. Later that night, Hal confessed to his son that we came in "DFL." Grant sailed with the team at Tufts University and was embarrassed to learn that his dad not only lost, but wore a Tufts sweatshirt in the race.

We were honored to attend Lee Wilson's wedding in the chapel at the U.S. Naval Academy in August 1992. Hal, a retired minister, presided over the celebration. It was a formal military ceremony that was enhanced with flashing sabers, due to Scott's rank as an officer.

107

Following the service, a bagpiper led the wedding party and invitees up the street to the Maryland Inn for the reception.

When Aunt Tib was visiting from Savannah in January 2003, we agreed to drive to Maryland to see her. Tib told stories that none of us, including her daughter, had heard before. In her 90s, she was extremely mentally alert: she read without glasses and played bridge. In the ensuing years, I often drove Marilyn to Savannah to visit her Mother who was now in an assisted living facility. Tib lived to be 107.

Beginning in 1987, we drove repeatedly to Connecticut, about a five-hour drive from Center City, to be with Bud's father and Dottie. We arrived either at Twin Lakes, near Canaan, where the Noble cottage was located, or Dottie's home, in Simsbury. We worked hard, with Mase, to maintain the lake property, and Bud had the good fortune to enjoy quality time with his father. After Mase's death in December 1997, the care of the cottage fell mainly on us. Visiting Dottie continued to be a major priority. She was a delightful person and we cherished her friendship. Our Christmas gift to her each year was providing and preparing the holiday dinner until she moved to McLean Senior Living.

Bud and I allotted considerable time to the care of the cottage. It was built in the early 1900s and therefore required much effort to maintain it. Along with his sisters Ann, Penny and Cathy, we devoted many hours to its upkeep. On trips to Twin Lakes, I met Bud's relatives that used the cottage or lived in the vicinity. Spending time with Bud's cousins usually provided an enlightening fact or two about family history.

One weekend at Twin Lakes, Sally Prestele (Dottie's sister) was next door at the Mather cottage that she owned with Dottie. She and two friends that were staying with her, along with Bud and me, hiked a portion of the Appalachian Trail surrounded by mountain laurel that was in full bloom. Sally hiked the trail in her bare feet! We were able to see Twin Lakes and the Noble cottage from atop Bear Mountain.

We enjoyed our first and only bona fide vacation at Twin Lakes in June 2001. Mother, Karen and Sue joined us. Dottie was next door at her cottage. It was a relaxing, enjoyable respite. Sue helped us put in the dock that became a comical undertaking watching Bud bob up and down under water as he attempted to level the dock by placing large rocks under supports. At times, we laughed so hard that we could not work.

Mother was surprised by the abundant vegetation and lack of shoulders along many highways in Connecticut and Massachusetts. She enjoyed the Norman Rockwell Museum in Stockbridge, Massachusetts, an hour's drive from Twin Lakes. She saw many Rockwell illustrations that she remembered from the covers of the *Saturday Evening Post*, a magazine that she subscribed to for many years.

After a week at Twin Lakes, Sue returned to Minnesota while the rest went to Pennsylvania. I bought Amtrak tickets for Mother and Karen to travel from Hartford to Philadelphia where they stayed at Karen's. A few days later, they joined us in Malvern. We took Mother to Valley Forge National Park, a place she found fascinating with its historic buildings, wildlife — deer were always visible — and beautiful vistas. We wandered through Amish countryside in Lancaster County, stopping to watch men working in the fields with teams of mules or to admire the neat rows of crops. We saw children selling produce and baked goods. Repeatedly, we slowed for a horse-drawn buggy.

Bud and I built a new cedar dock for the cottage in June 2003. Bud's design required making three platforms, several sections leading out to the platforms at the end of the dock and new supports. It was a major undertaking, perhaps a bit overkill, with the large platforms. It was met with overwhelming approval, including a "very impressive" comment from a neighbor. The next spring, we converted the three platforms into four smaller ones to make them more manageable.

Cedar dock built by Bud and David – June 2003

We made several trips to "The Land of 10,000 Lakes" that included celebrations of Vivian's 95th (2006) and 100th (2011) birthdays. Our first two trips to Minnesota included lengthy stays at Lake of the Woods. In July 1988 Jim met us at MSP Airport (Minneapolis-Saint Paul), and from there drove us directly to the Peterson cabins. We were joined by his girlfriend, Linda, Bob and Les, James Scott and Mother. Minnesota was suffering from a drought that left the lake level very low. It was difficult entering the boats from the pier high above the water. Boating through narrow passageways required us to proceed with caution because of the shallow water.

James Scott accompanied us on the long drive from Baudette to Sauk Centre. We stopped at Black Duck to see a huge replica of a black duck representing the city's namesake. Our next stop was Lake Itasca State Park to see the headwaters of the Mississippi River. Bud stepped from stone-to-stone as he made his way across the beginning of that river. James insisted that we stop at a Dairy Queen to introduce us to

"Blizzards." I have been hooked on them ever since. In Sauk Centre, Bud had an opportunity to see where I spent my childhood. We had coffee at the historic Palmer House and boated the length of Sauk Lake.

Our second trip to the North Star State was over Labor Day 1991. We returned to Lake of the Woods with the water back to normal level. Good weather made it possible to cross the lake into Canada. We had lunch on an island and later stopped for ice cream in Kenora. En route, we saw three black bears in the water that quickly swam to shore. We covered approximately 200 nautical miles on that day-long trip. Another day, we relaxed on beautiful Pine Island, not far from Jim's cabin. We watched two adult bald eagles sitting on a nest with their fledgling.

We refused to pass up an incredible bargain in 2001: a week in Spain at a five-star hotel arranged through Siemen's travel agency. Our time was devoted mostly to the sights and sounds of Madrid. Twice, we had lunch at La Cervecería Alemana, the pub where Cris, Jim and I imbibed several times in 1972. Since it was Bud's first time to Madrid, we fulfilled the obligatory visit to El Prado Museum and an afternoon of relaxation in El Retiro Park. We found time for side trips to Segovia — a World Heritage site — and Toledo. The Moorish fortress at Segovia impressed us the most because of its architecture and prominent location on a precipice. A portion of a Roman aqueduct and the cathedral are two other impressive landmarks. Toledo, as I described earlier in travels with Frank, is an interesting city with its many historical sites.

We managed a trip to Amsterdam in mid-winter, another benefit of Siemens travel agency. We found the architecture very curious: houses along the canals are narrow with big narrow windows, gable tops and a pulley outside to transport larger objects to upper floors. The food, with its Indonesian flavors, was much to our liking. We used the canal water taxis, a good way to relax and, at the same time, observe the architecture.

One year, Santa Fe, New Mexico was a Christmas destination to visit Bud's friend Mark. We strolled down streets lined with *luminarias,* stopping occasionally for a complimentary libation offered by local merchants or to listen to carolers. Mark drove us to Bandelier National Monument near Los Alamos. The monument preserves the homes and territory of the Ancestral Puebloans, dating between 1150 and 1600 CE. We climbed ladders into the ancient Indian cliff dwellings. On Christmas Day, we witnessed the famous Navajo Deer Dance in Taos.

We returned to the Southwest in December 2001, this time to Palm Springs and Tucson. Steve Guarnaschelli was our host in Palm Springs. One morning, we drove to Idyllwild in the mountains above Palm Springs. Relaxation was poolside with Steve or Doris, his Dachshund.

From Steve's, we drove from California to Arizona to meet Bill Haller. We stayed overnight at a property in Phoenix that his company managed, then left early the next morning for the Grand Canyon. The primary purpose of our trip was to spread the ashes of Steve Hall (who died the previous year) over the canyon wall. The Grand Canyon represented a special place, for them. They routinely stayed at the ranch on the canyon floor.

Bill reserved a cabin on the canyon rim. We arrived in time to see the sunset, a dramatic event at one of nature's masterpieces. Dinner was accompanied with aromatic mesquite wood fires burning throughout the lodge. The building was tastefully decorated for Christmas. Overnight, a storm left behind more than a foot of snow. We woke to a winter wonderland. The snow did not keep us from walking around, nor from spreading Steve's ashes. Reluctantly, we packed our bags for Bill's home in Tucson. Our timing was perfect. We followed directly behind a snowplow as it opened the impassable road.

In September 2002 we flew to Minnesota to attend the wedding reception of my niece Lori Lynn Schurman. Lori married Jeffrey Peterson (no relation) a few weeks earlier. The reception, hosted by the Vances in Redwood Falls, went off like clockwork. As a young girl, Lori Lynn came to Dallas to visit Karen and me. When in high school, Lori and her mother came to Philadelphia. On a hot and humid Atlantic coast summer day, I drove them to Washington, D.C. to see some of the monuments and tour the Capitol building and Washington Cathedral.

Washington, D.C. was a common destination, for Bud and me. In 1987, we joined Dallas friends in the Texas contingent for the March on Washington. Two years later, we returned to see the massive AIDS Memorial Quilt. We were distressed to see names, photos and stories of friends artfully sewn onto quilts. Bud's cousin Jean provided accommodations in her Arlington home whenever we were in Washington. We sometimes had lunch at the Hawk and Dove on Capitol Hill. We did that on separate occasions with Tim Clark, my brothers and Jim Bucko. We were in D.C. to celebrate Thanksgiving with associates that I met earlier in the year in Louisiana during Hurricane Katrina disaster relief work.

In 2011, we attended a very memorable funeral at Arlington National Cemetery for Bud's cousin John Martinez, a commandant in the U.S. Coast Guard. A procession led by a U.S.C.G. color guard, marching unit and band was followed by a rider-less horse and a caisson pulled by 8 black horses. Taps and a gun salute added to the somber moment at the grave site. Coincidentally, my brother Jim knew John when they were associated with the Coast Guard Academy.

We finally accepted an invitation from Joe Steiniger to spend a long weekend at his cabin near Schroon Lake, New York. On Presidents' Day 2004, we loaded our Jeep and drove up the New York State Thruway to the Adirondacks. 4WD was required to maneuver the snow-covered mountain roads. We arrived late Friday evening after a seven-hour drive. Joe built much of the cabin on weekends over a period of several years. The dwelling was cozy and nicely decorated. The setting on Bullet Pond, surrounded by trees and wildlife, was serene and beautiful.

The weekend was full of activity. On Saturday, we participated in the Saranac Lake Winter Carnival. Bud walked the circumference of Bullet Pond with Chuck following behind in his path. Joe invited four others to join us that evening for a tasty dinner. Everyone was impressed with his cooking. The next morning, the temperature had plunged to negative 17 degrees. Chuck's paws were only able to tolerate the cold for a few minutes.

We returned to England in September 2004 to see Margaret and Roy Mole in their new home. Two years earlier, they moved from Surrey to Goring-By-Sea on the English Channel. The beach was only a half-mile walk from their home. As to be expected, they were gracious hosts. The south of England offered many new places to explore: Worthing, Highdown Gardens, Bosham and Rustington, to name a few. Bud and I took day trips, easily reached by train, to Portsmouth and Chichester. When we were not sightseeing, we went to a pub or local restaurant or simply sat in their beautiful English garden.

After a hiatus of nearly 30 years, I returned to *la República de Panamá* in March 2005, with Bud accompanying me. For two weeks, we resided with Alex and Emita Cantón. It was a special time as we renewed our friendships. Everyone immediately accepted Bud and, for him, communication was not a problem, as most Panamanians had a command of English. Akim and Vadim Cantón, two of their sons, were often in our company. We ate most meals *en casa* (at home), savoring the delicious food prepared by Emita.

The four of us drove to El Valle, a quaint little mountain village located in the crater of an extinct volcano not far from Panama City. Thanks to altitude, the climate is moderate all year. We ate *comida típica* (Panamanian cuisine) prepared by a chef in a local restaurant. We walked around a zoo that housed native species and shopped at the local market. One day, we took a launch to Taboga Island and devoured a meal of fresh fish, the best seafood meal during our stay in Panamá!

We were in Panamá for the birth of Diego Alejandro Cantón, first child of Vadim and Nuny (Valeria). It was an honor to be included in that intimate event held in a hospital room with a champagne toast. Vadim was overwhelmed and speechless, so Alex spoke on his behalf.

Akim and Kathy invited us to dine in their home where their precocious daughter, Sara, entertained us. Kathy, a real estate agent, gave me a tour of several new high-rise condominiums that have sprung up in Panama's skyline. The city was certainly different from when I lived there, resembling coastal cities of Florida.

Penny and Eileen, Bud's sister and partner, coordinated a trip to Panamá with ours. Eileen was born in the Canal Zone. This was her first time to return to Panamá since graduating from Balboa High School in 1960! Together, we explored Panama City and its environs. We wandered through streets of *Casco Viejo,* the location of the former *Hotel Colonial* where I was first housed as a Peace Corps volunteer. I was surprised to see that the *Colonial* had been converted to an upscale condominium. We ventured into the former Canal Zone, now mostly a residential area, and Eileen discovered her childhood home. We hiked through *Parque Metropolitano* (Metropolitan Park). The park is situated on the Panama Canal's eastern shore and is home to dozens of species of mammals, birds, reptiles, amphibians and trees.

Alex and Emita gave Bud and me two *taguas* (detailed figurines hand carved from a nut of the *tagua* tree by indigenous people of the Darién) as *recuerdos* (gifts, memories) of Panamá. The *taguas* were a tortoise and an iguana. To express gratitude and leave a memory of my visit, I requested Vadim to photograph Alex, Emit and me. He had it framed and gift wrapped.

Alex, Emita and David – March 2005 – Panamá

When Bud returned to Philadelphia, I joined Penny and Eileen in the mountain village of Boquete where we stayed at the Villa Marita Lodge. We rafted down the *Rio Esti,* surrounded by abundant wildlife and colorful fauna, spotting several iguana and exotic birds. Only Eileen fell from the raft into the river when we encountered swirling white water. The area offered river rafting available up to an extreme level, depending on the location and amount of precipitation. Ours was a humble level 2.

There were remarkable changes in Panamá since my Peace Corps days. A huge building boom had occurred: new commercial buildings, multiple story condominiums, new highways and wonderful restaurants. The entire area that once comprised the U.S. Canal Zone had been converted into a residential area. The Panama Canal was run successfully and profitably by Panamanians. The foreign influx from Europe, South and North America was substantial. AARP, among other organizations, considers Panamá an ideal place to retire.

I arranged to visit the current Peace Corps office. It was in a high-rise building with security and a huge staff, all with personal computers. Jean Lujan, PC Country Director, informed me that there were no records or photos of groups prior to the reinstatement of the Peace Corps in Panamá in 1991. PCVs were now permitted to return to the States during their tour and each was issued a mobile phone. To me, it was a total shock as I reflected on my experience of the 1960s. Times had changed! Afterwards, I invited several PCVs to join me for lunch.

Sorrowfully, not long after our visit, Alex informed us that Emita was in a coma following a massive brain hemorrhage. She died several months later in July 2006. We were fortunate to have had a wonderful holiday with them while Emita was healthy.

Akim Cantón wrote a simple, beautiful eulogy that he read aloud at his mother's funeral. The translation from Spanish to English is mine.

Thank you all for coming and sharing in our goodbye to my mother, Emita Cantón.

Alex, Emita, Vadim, Pipo, Akim and Tita [Emita's mother] always viewed our family as perfect, and my mother was the bond that united it. For that reason, the past year has been very difficult for everyone because we lost the "captain" of our team.

Everyone who knew Mother will treasure hundreds of her memories that will continue to follow us. All are joyous, full of goodness, happy, bright and loving. My father always says to treasure those memories, and that is what we will do: laugh at her stories, apply her wise advice and live according to what she taught us.

We understand that nothing will be the same as before, and that our family will never be the unit that it was, but mother will continue to influence every step and decision of our lives, and one day we will see her and once again be the perfect family.

117

June 2006 was a travel month with visits to Seattle — after more than twenty years — and a first to Victoria, British Columbia. Cris LeGassey hosted me in Seattle. No matter how long in between, we simply pick up where we left off. We drove over the mountains to Ellensburg and down the Yakima River Valley — wine country — in eastern Washington.

I made a voyage from Seattle to Victoria aboard the *Victoria Clipper*. Bruce Dutton and I covered every inch of that city and its surroundings. Although Bruce was born in Victoria, he lived in Devon, Pennsylvania much of his life. He taught French and Spanish at The Agnes Irwin School, a non-sectarian college preparatory day school for girls in Bryn Mawr, Pennsylvania. He moved back to Victoria after he retired. Bud and I knew Bruce well. He lived within a few miles of our Malvern home and was a mutual friend of Bob and Lee.

Participation in English immersion courses in Spain, Germany and Hungary — through Diverbo and Angloville — introduced me to new opportunities in 2013, 2014 and 2015. Those intensive seven-day courses were for people who already had a knowledge of English but wanted to improve their conversational ability. The programs were voluntary for instructors (I paid my own transportation to the venues) but all expenses were covered during the program, including room and board, and the facilities were of 5-star quality. In 2013, once I completed the course in Spain, I remained in the country to visit friends in Alicante.

I participated in the last two programs with Tim Clark: the first in the Black Forest of Germany and the second in Budapest. Following the German program, we spent several days in Munich. Before the Hungarian program, we were in Prague and Vienna, and after the program, we enjoyed a week in Budapest. I consider Prague and Budapest — World Heritage Sites — to be the most beautiful cities in the world. Budapest, in spite of its size, has many attractions and is ideally located on the banks of the Danube River.

Mason Noble V and David Peterson
First toast – wedding day – December 14, 2014

Chapter 18

THE LAST HURRAH

We gladly returned to Philadelphia after Bud retired in 2015. We rented an apartment at the historic Touraine, on Spruce Street. That year was used to find a place that would hopefully meet our needs for the rest of our lives. It was always our plan to enjoy our last years in Philly. With Bud's persistent research and help from our agent Samantha, we found a unit at the William Penn House (WPH).

Prior to our move, we had to sell our townhome. To our surprise, our real estate agents told us that our home did not require any staging and was immediately ready to go on the market. We had maintained it well and it sold in a short time. Our immediate task was to downsize from nearly 2400 square feet to 1200 square feet, more or less, for a city dwelling. Many items had served their purpose for 30 years; hence, we were willing to part with them.

WPH is a cooperative located in Center City on Chestnut Street next to Rittenhouse Square. It is a large building with 31 floors, one block long and 275 feet tall. The number of units is approaching 500, as owners continue to buy adjacent apartments to combine with theirs. Amenities include a rooftop pool, gym, community room with a library, 24-hour security and a rental car company on the premises. The property is well maintained and affordable in a prime area of the city.

Our two-bedroom unit is on the 12th floor. Although partially renovated by prior owners, it required several upgrades: new kitchen plumbing, painting, kitchen cabinets, a vanity to the bath, lowering all lintels and replacing all doors. Our second bedroom was converted to a den, library and TV room. Our favorite asset is a 6 by 20-foot balcony that we adorn with plants, a table and chairs and a hammock.

WPH residents are various ages, ethnicities, professions and religions and reflect the diversity of Philadelphia. They are an appealing aspect to our home. We have become acquainted with many neighbors and share reciprocal favors with some. The maintenance and security staff are cordial and helpful. There are monthly events in the community room.

Shortly after moving into WPH, we were asked by a neighbor to participate in the Center City Residents Association annual house tour. Soon, we found ourselves committee members. Bud created and managed a spreadsheet to coordinate the CCRA volunteers. I interviewed homeowners and wrote synopses of their houses for the brochure. During the process we met influential people, gained more knowledge of the City and viewed several impressive residences.

We continue to be unwavering spokesmen for Center City and eagerly serve as guides to our visitors. Philly is a residential city steeped in history. There are hundreds of diverse restaurants, renowned museums, the Philadelphia Orchestra, beautiful squares and parks and countless historic attractions. After all, this is where America began! There is access to excellent transportation. We are familiar with the buses, trolleys, subway, El, regional rail system and Amtrak. A big bonus for senior citizens is that most public transportation is free.

As I was bringing my story to a close in the fall of 2020, Covid-19 (a coronavirus) has changed our lives — and the world's — significantly. Initially, the entire city of Philadelphia was virtually shut down except for "essential businesses." The streets were desolate save for emergency vehicles, creating an eerie silence. Social or physical distancing has become the new normal, along with wearing masks and isolating when necessary. Activities are limited to grocery shopping or taking walks for a breath of fresh air. Hundreds of thousands have died and the death toll continues to rise. This unprecedented pandemic defies a prediction.

I have confronted other troubling issues recently as well. Politics is one. Not a day goes by that I am not affected — stressed — by the nation's political situation. Hopefully, the future will bring about a more responsible federal government and "normalcy" will be restored. Another is the economy that has suffered greatly as a result of the pandemic. A third is the turbulence across the nation brought on by the loss of lives in the black community. The awareness of racism by the general public is a positive result. In my lifetime, there has been a considerable downward trend in the respect for others, or even life, for that matter. I would like to see values in society restored. They need to be taught in schools and stressed at home.

My mother's assessment of me having "a mind of his own" has definitely come true. I have always followed my heart and let things fall into place and, for the most part, things have fallen positively. I would recommend that advice to everyone, above all, young people who have their lives ahead of them. We — as individuals — have the ability to create much of our own success. However, I do believe that fate can play a role, consequently, some things cannot be predicted but they can be controlled or overcome. I believe that my personal secret to happiness is living life to the fullest but responsibly. At the same time, it is important to be sincere, genuine and honest.

I have no regrets to the varied occupational road I followed. On the contrary, diversity only added to my personal growth and satisfaction. It also led to meeting people from all walks of life and, subsequently, imparted an appreciation and understanding of them. One of the most important things I have learned is to nurture friendships. It may require an effort to reach out to them. True friends are rare and are to be treasured.

ADDENDUM

Peterson Family Tree
(Includes two generations of immediate family)

FATHER – (1) <u>Edward Carl Peterson</u> was the oldest of four children (born 13Mar1909, died 13Jan1999). Ed married Vivian Jane Coons on 17Nov1935 in Sauk Centre, Stearns County, Minnesota in a private ceremony with two friends as witnesses.
Children of Edward and Vivian:

    <u>James Edward Peterson</u> (born 15May1937, died 05Sep2019), married Gail Gruse Nelson.
    <u>Karen Jane Peterson</u> (born 30Nov1940)
    <u>David Carol Peterson</u> (born 22Nov1943), married Mason Noble V (born 23Sep1948) on 16Dec2014 in Exton, Chester County, Pennsylvania.
    <u>Carol Sue Peterson</u> (born 19Dec1946) married Donald Vance.
    <u>Robert Lowell Peterson</u> (born 19Dec1946) married Nancy Rasmussen.

(2) Ethel Lucille Peterson (born 12Jun1914, died 21May2004) married Orvylle William Johnson
    Kathleen Ardys Johnson
    Janet Larinda Johnson Izzo

(3) Arthur Donald Peterson (born 15Jan1920, died 31Dec1962) married Lucille Levernz.
    Donald Peterson
    Lawrence Peterson
    Kay Peterson

(4) Dorothy Marie Peterson (born 08May1922, died 13Oct1977) married Harry Freedland.
>David Jack Freedland
>Thomas Dale Freedland

Grandparents – Olaf Peterson (born 18Oct1873, died 12Nov1957) married Leah Ada Drager on 03Sep1906 in Little Sauk, Todd County, Minnesota.
>Leah Ada Drager (born 10Sep1885, died 30Oct1933)

MOTHER – (2) Vivian Jane Coons (born 01Jan1911, died 20Mar2012) was the second of two children.

(1) Carol Winfield Coons (born 16Feb1907, died 02Mar1986) married Isabel Caldwell Hansen (born 25Jul1909, died 11Aug2016).
>Marilyn Ann Coons Wilson
>Joan Isabel Coons Mahaney
>Carol Jean Coons Morris

Grandparents – Ulysses James Coons (born 22Jun1872, died 04Jan1946) married Arvilla Elizabeth Lamb on 17Jun1902 in Sauk Centre, Stearns County, Minnesota.
>Arvilla Elizabeth Lamb (born 15Feb1873, died 04May1961)

George Majors

(The words below are inscribed on the tombstone of George Majors at the National Cemetery in Fairfax, Vermont)

George Majors

In memory of George Majors who died August 28, 1842, aged 100 years. He was a native of Germany. He came to America in Burgoyne's army and deserted at Ticonderoga and joined the American army at Bennington, Vermont, a volunteer. He was a faithful Republican and served during the revolutionary war. At the close of the war he married and settled in Sunderland, Vermont. From thence he moved to Essex and from thence to Fairfax in 1800 where he spent the remainder of his days an industrious farmer and true Christian.

His wife

In memory of Mrs. Barsheba Majors who died April 01, 1822 in the 73 year of her age, wife of George Majors. "Blessed are the dead which died in the Lord from henceforth yea sayth the spirit that they may rest from their labors and their works do follow thence." Rev 14 – 15

(George Majors was David Peterson's great-great-great-great-great-grandfather, related to him through his father's mother, Leah Ada Drager.)

David Peterson

DESCRIPTION OF PEACE CORPS VOLUNTEER SERVICE

CUERPO DE PAZ
U.S. PEACE CORPS
CALLE 41 ESTE NO. 3
PANAMA, R. DE P.

David C. Peterson – Volunteer No. 191542 – Panama

Mr. David C. Peterson entered training on July 16, 1967 at Camp David Crozier, Arecibo, Puerto Rico and completed an intensive ten-week program. Included in the subjects studied were Spanish, Panamanian History, Cooperatives, Economics and Investigation of Barriada Problems.

He was enrolled in the Peace Corps on October, 1967. Upon arrival in Panama, Mr. Peterson participated in a five-week orientation program at Desarrollo Comunal Urbano (Urban Community Development) in Panama City. He was responsible to the Instituto para la Formacion y Aprovechamiento de Recursos Humanos (IFARHU), an autonomous government agency during his service in Panama. Mr. Peterson served as an occupational counselor assigned to the Centro Nacional de Aprendizaje (National Apprenticeship Center). As a Peace Corps Volunteer and Occupational Counselor, he worked in professional training at three levels: semi-skilled, skilled and professional. This position involved the selection and follow-up procedures of the personnel related to the three above mentioned groups and included the following duties: interviewing, psychological testing, selection, supervision and counseling of students.

Additionally, he attended the XII Interamerican Psychology Congress, March 30 – April 06, 1969 in Montevideo, Uruguay as a delegate of IFARHU. He visited the countries of Chile, Argentina, Uruguay, Bolivia, Peru and Colombia.

Pursuant to section 5 (f) of the Peace Corps Act, 22 U.S.C.S 2504 (f), as amended, any former Volunteer employed by the United States Government following his Peace Corps Volunteer service is entitled to have any period of satisfactory Peace Corps Volunteer service credited for purposes of retirement, seniority, reduction in force, leave and other privileges based on length of Government service.

This is to certify in accordance with Executive Order No. 11103 of April 10, 1963, that Mr. David C. Peterson served satisfactorily as a Peace Corps Volunteer. His service ended on August 20, 1969. His benefits under the Executive Order extend for a period of one year after termination of Volunteer service, except that the employing agency may extend the period for up to three years for a former Volunteer who enters military service of pursues studies at a recognized institution of higher education.

Signed by John B Arango
Peace Corps Director/Panama
August 20, 1969

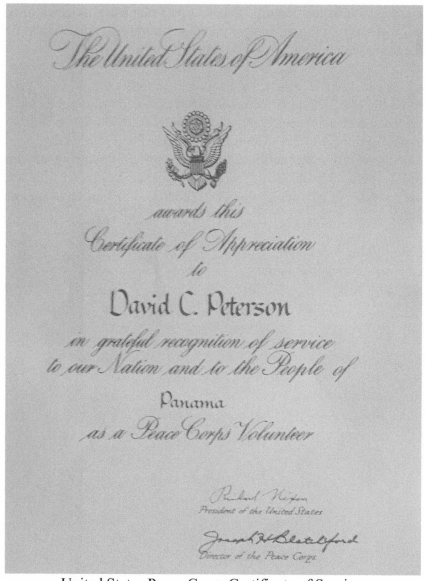

United States Peace Corps Certificate of Service

DESCRIPTION OF CRISIS CORPS VOLUNTEER SERVICE

Disaster Recovery Effort – Hurricane Katrina 2005
Marksville, Louisiana

DATES OF SERVICE: 08 September to 07 October, 2005

NAME: <u>David C. Peterson</u>

SSN: xxx-xx-xxxx

COUNTRY: United States, Group 1

STATE: Louisiana

POSITION TITLE: Applicant Services Specialist in the Individual Assistance Cadre

I.   Description of training:

Conducted at the Federal Emergency Management Agency's training center in Orlando, Florida, **David Peterson** received training in the functions of Disaster Recovery Centers including tracking the status of applications via web-based programs, providing referrals and mitigation information, and problem resolution. **David** also received training in Equal Employment Opportunity Commission standards and Safety and Security in the field.

Upon graduation from the center, **David Peterson** was able to assist with web-based applications; routing applicants to appropriate services; providing authoritative information, explanations, program requirements and referrals to applicants affected by disasters, and assist in case processing and program eligibility decisions.

<u>David Peterson</u> was sworn in as a Crisis Corps Volunteer on **<u>09 September 2005</u>**.

II.   Description of assignment:

Following training **David Peterson** was deployed to Baton Rouge, Louisiana. At the Joint Field Office of FEMA **<u>David</u>** was assigned to Disaster Recovery Center

(DRC) #2 in Marksville, Avoyelles Parish, Louisiana as an Applicant Services Representative. At the DRC he worked with volunteers from various agencies, FEMA employees, and personnel from other support groups. In his position he met one-on-one with evacuees from Hurricanes Katrina and Rita with the primary purpose of providing information and requirements of the individual assistance programs for which they were eligible.

The most important responsibilities involved accessing the individual records of the applicants in the FEMA software database and verifying the accuracy of that information, making necessary corrections, additions and updates; assisting the applicant to resolve specific issues; referring the applicant to other assistance programs, community resources and other appropriate agencies; reviewing the applicant status to determine eligibility for financial and direct assistance, then forwarding it to the National Processing Service Center; and determining the applicant's immediate and long-term housing needs.

III.   Achievements:

David Peterson became very proficient in the FEMA web-based applications and knowledgeable of FEMA programs. He was initially one of two volunteers at the center who had a PC and access to the FEMA website. **David** was selected as a trainer to cross train others at the DRC and train new staff toward the end of his assignment. As a fluent Spanish speaker, he was called on occasionally to assist speakers of that language. **David**, along with other volunteers, helped set up the DRC the day before opening. The manager of the DRC provided a very positive Performance Review and Recommendation in appreciation of his service.

IV.   Primary Project: Katrina Louisiana Disaster Recovery, DRC #2, Marksville, Louisiana

David Peterson served as an Applicant Services Representative interviewing the applicants to ensure they received the benefits to which they were entitled. The data collected was entered on a FEMA personal computer.

V.   Other experiences:

David Peterson witnessed firsthand the arrival of Hurricane Rita on 22 and 23 September, but fortunately his area was spared major damage and the DRC was only closed one day. **David** worked one day with the US Public Health Service at the Lamar-Dixon Animal Shelter in Gonzales, LA, monitoring the area from a health perspective and recommending changes to make it safe for the workers.

VI.   Comments on physical demands of the position, if any:

David Peterson, along with most of the DRC staff, was housed in the nearby community of Bunkie. He commuted daily about 15 miles each way to and from the DRC in Marksville. The DRC staff reported at 0700 each morning and worked until 1900, or later if necessary, to accommodate the evacuees. For three nights **David** lived in a tent city near Baton Rouge before his deployment to the DRC.

PRIVACY ACT NOTICE/NON-COMPETITIVE ELIGIBILITY

The information requested herein is collected pursuant to Section 5 of the Peace Corps Act (USC 2504 (f)). The information will be used exclusively to prepare the Description of Volunteer Service Statement, which will be permanently retained by the Peace Corps. The statement will be used to verify service performed.

This is to certify in accordance with Executive Order No. 11103 of 10 April 1963 that **David C. Peterson** served satisfactorily as a Peace Corps Volunteer. His service ended on **07 October 2005**.

Pursuant to Section 5(f) of the Peace Corps Act, 22 USC No. 2504 (f) as amended, any former Volunteer employed by the United States government following his /her Peace Corps Service is entitled to have any period of satisfactory Peace Corps Volunteer Service based on length of government service. Peace Corps service shall not be credited toward completion of a probationary p0r trial period or completion of any service requirement for career appointment.

NOTE: Presidential directive establishing non-competitive eligibility in 1963 after completion of at least one year of Peace Corps service; see Federal Personnel Manual (FPM), Chapter 315, 6-7. Therefore, service under the Katrina Relief Initiative does not qualify.

Signed by Mary Angelini, 21 March 2006
Director of the Crisis Corps

David Peterson

A note of thanks is owed to Joe Roy who helped modify the written material. He offered many suggestions to improve the content, including the addition of photos. Without his encouragement, the outcome would have been mundane, at best. Any shortcomings are mine, as I made additions and changes after I received Joe's draft. Above all, I am grateful for Bud Noble's love, patience and support.

A Mind of his Own

Made in the USA
Las Vegas, NV
04 April 2021